The Evolution of Dog Training

From choke chains
to clickers, uncovering
the secrets to having a
well-behaved dog.

Shannon Coyner

Truly Force Free Animal Training
Ventura, California

Interior Design: J. L. Saloff
Cover Design: Mark Saloff Designs
Photos from Wikipedia Commons:
Skinner box image, adapted from Boite skinner.jpg
Puppy Mill, public domain from PETA
Flickr Photo: Paul Englefield, "Weave":
www.flickr.com/photos/hawksanddoves/244517659/

Copyright information available upon request. v. 1.02

Print ISBN: 978-0-9992846-0-5
E-book ISBN: 978-0-9992846-1-2
Library of Congress Number: 2017914263

Published in the United States of America on acid-free paper.

First Edition

To my children: Riley, Shawn, and Cole.
If you live your passion and follow your inspirations,
your dreams will come true.

A special thank you to my husband, Jeff.
Without his encouragement and support,
this book would not exist.

Contents

Forward

My parents adopted Tammy before I was born. She was a beautiful fawn female Staffordshire Bull Terrier. My parents loved that dog and bred her one time. At about the same time, my parents decided to start a family. Tammy had her litter of four roly-poly puppies on Mother's Day. I was born three months later.

Three of the puppies went to other homes, but my parents kept one whom we named Spike. I grew up with Spike. He was my best friend and playmate as a child. I still remember sitting in the back yard with him taking turns licking my ice cream cones.

Spike loved everyone in my family, but he desperately adored my mom. When my mom would leave the house, Spike would cry and whine uncontrollably. Like most dog handlers of that time, my parents tried scolding and punishing Spike to stop this behavior. It did not work. I did not understand that Spike was suffering from separation anxiety. I only knew that when my mom left, he was desperately unhappy and I wished I could help him.

By the time I reached high school, Tammy and Spike had passed away. My family adopted a yellow Labrador puppy we named Missy. Missy was a playful puppy, and just about as sweet as could be. I decided to take Missy through obedience classes. Like every obedience class at that time, using a choke chain to train Missy was mandatory. When she made a mistake, the trainer said to correct her by "popping" her (pulling up on the leash quickly so the chain would "pop" and quickly tighten around her neck). The idea was to cause pain, so she would stop making the mistake.

Although I used it, I was very uncomfortable with the choke chain. At one point, Missy was being a little wild, like most young lab puppies, and the trainer suggested I use a pinch collar. Even as a teenager I wanted to get away from using pain as much as possible, so I refused. I decided to practice more without the choke chain instead. I woke up as the sun came up every morning before school to practice. Missy eventually could sit, stay, and heel perfectly off leash. She ended up being one of the most obedient dogs my parents ever had.

As an adult, I adopted my first two dogs with my husband; Sadi, a jet black Flat Coat Retriever, and Buster, a rough coat, tri color Jack Russell Terrier. Although Sadi was both my husband's and my dog, Buster was essentially all mine. Buster was a smart, scruffy, bundle of energy and I loved evrything about him.

I joined an obedience class with Buster. Again, the teacher of the class asked that all the students use choke chains. I was still not comfortable with using the choke chain, but there were no classes in the area teaching anything different.

Being a high energy dog, Buster had a tendency to bark at other dogs during the class. Training instructions were to pop him when he barked. But these pops seemed to only make matters worse. Soon Buster was barking and growling at other dogs when they got close. Intuitively, I knew that the choke chain was making Buster's behavior worse.

As I attended the classes and practiced with Buster, I realized that the corrections were making him scared. The smart, confident terrier that I loved so much was becoming a bundle of nerves. He was not learning. I decided to drop out of that class and began researching other training techniques.

I had graduated from Sonoma State University with a Degree in Biology/Zoology, and I had also worked and volunteered in zoos by this time. There, I had a little exposure to positive training. I decided to look into using these techniques for my dogs. My research led me to books by animal behaviorists Dr. Ian Dunbar, Karen Pryor, and Dr. Karen Overall.

I started to use the positive techniques in the books. I quickly saw how Buster learned more, with less fear, using positive reinforcement methods. I became a Registered Veterinary Technician about this time and began to attend conferences focusing on animal behavior. I learned about the theories and scientific basis behind positive reinforcement training. I never used correction based training again.

Buster would be 21 if he were alive today. Twenty-one years ago, correction based training was still by far the most common training technique. I am so grateful that I was able to discover positive reinforcement. As a positive reinforcement trainer, I am a smarter, kinder, and more compassionate person.

My mission for this book (and any other animal book I write), my training center (Ventura Pet Wellness and Dog

Training) and my training website (Truly Force Free Animal Training—trulyforcefree.com) is quite simple: I want to educate people around the world that you do not need to use force, pain, or manipulation to teach an animal. I also want everyone to realize that science has shown that dogs learn and process information much like we do. Although the outside of their bodies look different and some of their internal anatomy may differ from ours, their brains process fear and pain like humans. I believe they feel more human emotions as well, including happiness, sadness, and even love. As a scientist, I know we may never prove this since dogs cannot use verbal language, but I know it without any doubts.

My journey taught me that taking the path less traveled is more work, but if you follow your heart, you will end up in the intended place. As a positive reinforcement trainer, I am able to help far more animals than I would have as a traditional trainer.

Introduction

Today on television and the Internet, there are literally thousands of dog trainers giving different advice regarding dog training. Some trainers suggest only giving rewards to train, some trainers only suggest using corrections/punishments, and some trainers use both.

Many of these trainers have various theories about how and why their training techniques work. One group suggests that we should try to emulate how the wolves treat each other in packs. Another group applies concepts used in human psychology and learning theory. One thing is for sure: many trainers are extremely passionate about their views and at times the feuds between them can get downright nasty.

But how do we wade through all the information out there to find the truth about what are the most effective ways to train dogs? The answer is simple but not easy. We must try to take an unbiased look at what scientific research tells us about dog behavior and then apply that to how we train dogs.

Why Use Science to Search for the Truth?
Scientists use a system called the scientific method to try to solve problems or answer questions. They do this by creating

theories, testing the theories by collecting data or performing experiments, and then analyzing the results to determine if their theories were true.[1] By performing tests to see if their theories are correct, the scientific method minimizes the influence of bias or prejudice in the person performing the experiment.

Scientists are also trained to use standard procedures and criteria when they perform their experiments and will try to publish their results in scientific journals to disseminate their work. This way, other scientists can see what was done, comment on the results, and conduct their own experiments to expand upon the work of others. The ultimate goal is to continually understand the truth about how our world operates.

"Science is the search for truth, that is the effort to understand the world: it involves the rejection of bias, of dogma, of revelation, but not the rejection of morality."
Linus Pauling

Cognitive Bias and the Semmelweis Reflex

Even after scientists discover the truth, having people accept it is not always easy. Denying scientific data is not a "new" phenomena. People have been denying scientific data for about as long as science has existed, especially if they feel threatened by the results.[2] One early example of this took place in Europe in 1844. Ignaz Semmelweis was born in 1818 in Hungary.[3] He became a physician in 1844 and soon after, he became involved with the problem called puerperal fever, or childbed fever. Childbed fever is an infection of some part of the female reproductive organs following childbirth. The infection can invade the bloodstream and lymph system to cause septicemia (blood poisoning) and death. The disease had become a plague in Europe.

Semmelweis became a doctor at the start of the "golden age of the physician scientist."[4] Starting at this time, physicians were expected to have scientific training and had begun to understand that illness was not an imbalance caused by bad air or evil spirits. Instead, physicians started looking at anatomy and began testing different theories regarding diseases. As part of this process, they started to routinely perform autopsies and began collecting data.

Semmelweis was interested in finding out why so many women in maternity wards were dying from childbed fever. After significant testing, he theorized that doctors were spreading the disease to their patients. At this time, gloves were not used and doctors did not routinely wash their hands between patients. To test his theory, Semmelweis ordered his medical staff to start cleaning their hands and instruments not just with soap but with a chlorine solution. Chlorine happens to be one of the most effective disinfectants. When Semmelwies imposed his new cleaning standards, the death rate plummeted from 18.27 to 1.27 percent.[5] He eventually even published his findings.

You'd think everyone would have been thrilled when Semmelweis solved the problem of puerperal infection, but they weren't thrilled. For one thing, doctors were upset because Semmelweis' hypothesis made it look like they were the ones causing the deaths of these women. Additionally, he was proposing a significant change in the way physicians operated which was unpopular. Eventually, the doctors gave up the chlorine hand-washing. Semmelweis even lost his job. It took many years before his studies were re-examined and eventually accepted. It is hard to imagine the number of people who must have died in the meantime.

This outcome is so astonishing it has been given a name—*the Semmelweis Reflex*. This response describes the predisposition to deny new information that challenges our established views.[6] As humans, our personal experiences impact how we view new information, something called cognitive bias. Cognitive bias can lead ordinarily reasonable people to make some unreasonable decisions. *The Semmelweis Reflex* is one form of cognitive bias.

Another form of cognitive bias is information bias. This describes the inclination to seek out information that supports our own preconceived notions. Most people don't like to be wrong, so they surround themselves with people and information that confirm their beliefs.

Science, Bias and Dog Training

The potential for bias means we have to be very careful about how we look at much of the information regarding dog training. Currently, most available advice about dog training is based on anecdotal evidence (personal testimony from trainers regarding what has worked and not worked for them in the past). Anecdotal evidence is not inherently bad as it often serves as a starting point for us to create theories and test things scientifically.

However because of bias, we must be very careful about accepting anecdotal evidence as truth if there is no separate scientific proof to back it up. If a dog trainer has been using the same training methods for decades and his livelihood is based on those methods, the potential to have biased views about those techniques is very high. Those trainers will also be predisposed to reject or ignore research that tells them their methods are outdated or harmful. Additionally, most of us will be naturally attracted to the dog training techniques that we used in the past. If you grew up training your dog a certain way, right or wrong, you are more likely to be biased toward seeing the good and ignoring the bad about what you know.

Therefore, when you read this book and the references to the studies, you may have strong, emotional responses to some of the conclusions. For example, if you used an electronic collar to train your dog in the past, you may feel under attack by a study finding that electronic collars are emotionally harmful to dogs. But the goal of this book is not to make you feel guilty about what you did in the past or to label you as a dog abuser. The goal is to look at what we currently know about dog behavior to try to find the truth about the best way to train dogs now and in the future.

One

Understanding the World of Dog Training

A young couple, Mike and Jill, adopted their beautiful two-year-old white German Shepherd from a rescue. Meeka was extremely sweet and well-behaved unless she was left home alone. If Mike and Jill left her, she would whine and bark so severely they feared she might go through a window. Meeka also barked at dogs when she passed them on walks. Before coming to me, they had worked with a trainer claiming to be an expert with German Shepherds. The two main pieces of advice they received from that trainer were:

They had to use a choke chain to control her because the neck was the strongest part of the dog's body.

They needed to get a Nanny Cam that allowed them to yell at her when she whined when they were gone. This supposedly mimicked God.

Fortunately, Mike and Jill realized that these suggestions did not seem right and continued to search for another trainer. That is when they found me. I could not believe this advice, and regrettably they paid a lot of money for it.

Sadly, I often hear of trainers giving advice that appears made up with no real theoretical or scientific basis. In most places, at least at the time of the printing of this book, becoming a dog trainer requires no formal training or education. Therefore, uneducated trainers dispense a lot of misinformation. This is sad, because in the last twenty years, our scientific understanding of how dogs think, learn, and feel has greatly expanded.

We no longer have to guess at what training methods are most effective. Based on the scientific data, we can examine both how traditional training works and how positive reinforcement training works as well as how these trainings impact dogs. In particular, we now have enough information to understand how the use of pain and force negatively impacts a dog's ability to learn as compared to positive reinforcement based techniques. To understand these differences, we must first understand how these two training methods work. Let's begin by looking at the theories behind traditional training and positive reinforcement training and their origins.

Traditional, Correction Based Training

The basic philosophy of traditional trainers is to correct any unwanted behavior often using a leash correction or "pop" and then praise the appropriate behavior. For example, a traditional trainer may ask a dog to sit. If the dog continues to stand (an unwanted behavior), the trainer will administer a correction/punishment using a leash pop. Leash corrections then will continue until the dog does the wanted behavior by sitting. Shock collars are another tool often used by traditional trainers to achieve this result. The trainer then may praise the dog for sitting, but this does not always happen.

When a dog is resisting known behaviors, traditional trainers often tell their clients that the dog is challenging their dominance in the relationship and that the dog needs more discipline. They encourage handlers to become strong pack leaders or to become the "alpha" of their pack. This often means increasing the intensity and duration of the corrections until the dog submits. Some trainers go as far as recommending giving little or no affection or rewards at all during this process to reinforce the handler's dominance over their dog.

Correction-Based Traditional Trainers Quotations

"If you give your dog nothing but affection, then you're combining the lack of exercise problem with a lack of discipline and creating a situation in which your dog will take over the pack. Provide exercise and affection with no discipline, and you'll get a dog that will never listen to anyone." Cesar Millan[1]

"The bottom line is adopting a dog at four years old with a history of chasing critters, ignoring commands, pulling on leashes, barking at external stimuli, is going to be hard to impossible to reprogram with food rewards alone." Ed Frawley.[2]

Electric pinch collar

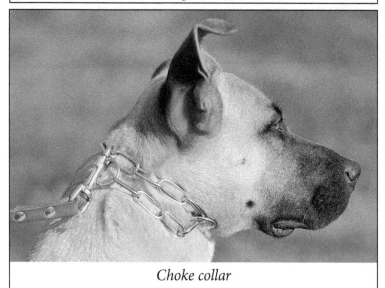

Choke collar

The Origins of Traditional Training

As I mentioned in the forward, I trained my first dog using both a choke chain and traditional training methods. Even as a teenager, I was uncomfortable with the harsh treatment. However, more than twenty years ago, correction based training was what most trainers used and people had been using these techniques for a very long time.

Many consider a German trainer named Colonel Konrad Most to be the father of modern traditional training . He authored a book entitled *Training Dogs, a Manual* in 1910. Colonel Most had a military background. He started training dogs while serving as Police Commissioner at the Royal Prussian Police headquarters in 1906. He later trained military dogs for Germany in World War I and World War II. From 1919 to 1937, he was head of the Canine Research Department of the Army High Command.

In his book, Colonel Most cautions that as dog trainers, we must resist our inclination to view our dogs anthropomorphically. He meant we should not think that our dogs respond emotionally, or that they think or otherwise act like humans. Colonel Most also strongly advocates correction based training methods and that the trainers must dominate over the dogs to ensure compliance with these corrections. As the book states:

> "In a pack of young dogs, fierce fights take place to decide how they are to rank within the pack. And in a pack composed of men and dogs, canine competition for importance in the eyes of the trainer is keen. If this state of affairs is not countered by

methods which the canine mind can comprehend, it frequently ends in such animals attacking and seriously injuring not only their trainers or other people. As in a pack of dogs, the order of hierarchy in a man and dog combination can only be established through physical force, that is by actual struggle, in which the man is instantly victorious. Such a result can only be brought about by convincing the dog of the absolute physical superiority of the man. Otherwise, the dog will lead and the man follow. If a dog shows the slightest sign of rebellion against his trainer or leader, the physical superiority of the man as leader of the pack gives instant expression in the most unmistakable manner."

"Should a dog rebel against his trainer, instant resort to severe compulsion [correction] is essential, for, each time the dog finds that it is not instantly mastered, the canine competitive instinct will increase and his submissive instinct will weaken."

In other words, dogs are physically and emotionally punished in order for a person to exercise superiority over the dog. If the dog rebels against his trainer—fights back or tries to protect himself—he will receive "severe compulsion"— aka, severe punishment. While the wording in Colonel Most's book is a bit more direct and harsh compared to the wording of more prominent correction based trainers today, the underlying theory is still clear. Unless dogs receive punishment using some form of physical correction or dominance, the dog will not consistently comply.

Most's training techniques spread throughout the world as his students immigrated to other countries. This included incorporation in the American Kennel Club and many other dog training institutions. One of Most's students, Carl Spitz, Sr., a German immigrant to the United States, helped train dogs in World War II for the United States.

Where the Alpha or Pack Theory Came From

Traditional trainers will also cite pack theory or alpha theory as a basis for their training technique. Rudolph Schenkel is generally regarded as the originator of this theory.[3] Schenkel was an animal behaviorist who, in 1947, published a paper Expressions Studies on Wolves. Schenkel studied captive wolves in Switzerland's Zoo in Basel in the 1930s and 1940s and wrote the paper attempting to identify a sociology of the wolf. Schenkel observed that when a group of wolves cohabited in a zoo setting, a hierarchy would develop and a head or alpha male along with an alpha female wolf would take over to dominate the rest of the pack. Throughout the paper, Schenkel drew parallels between wolves and domestic dogs leading to the conclusion that domesticated dogs also require a pack structure with an alpha male or female leading the group.

This research was next picked up by another researcher named L. David Mech who wrote a book in the late 1960s entitled *The Wolf: Ecology and Behavior of an Endangered Species*. The book was a synthesis of available wolf information at the time and included much of Schenkel's research.

Mech adopted Schenkel's alpha wolf terminology in the book. The book, published in 1970 and republished in 1981, sold over 120,000 copies.[4] It is generally credited for spreading the theory into widespread use.

However, as time went on, Mech began to distance himself from Schenkel's work. In the late 1990s after Mech lived with a wild pack of wolves on Ellesmere Island near the North Pole, Mech started to revise his thinking. He observed that most wolf packs are a family group with the parents at the top and the children following their lead.

> "Rather than viewing a wolf pack as a group of animals organized with a top dog that fought its way to the top, or a male-female pair of such aggressive wolves, science has come to understand that most wolf packs are merely family groups formed exactly the same way as human families are formed."[5]

The prior observations by Schenkel simply did not apply to wolves in the wild, as the wolves he studied lived in an artificial setting. Mech published these corrections in 1999, 2000, and again in 2009, noting that the term alpha wolf had been slowly disappearing from scientific papers and studies.[6]

Additionally, subsequent research into the behavior of dogs has further called into question the viability of dominance theory. For example, a study in 2009 investigated the interactions between a group of nineteen dogs living together.[7] The study investigated whether neutered domestic dogs formed a hierarchical structure as predicted by the dominance theory. Within the group, interactions between each pair of dogs were recorded. But by the conclusion of the study, no specific hierarchy between the dogs developed. In other words, no top alpha dog emerged to dominate all the other dogs. Instead, the relationship between the dogs appeared fluid and could vary depending on the circumstances and dogs.

Force Free, Positive Training

As opposed to using corrections, positive trainers seek to reinforce desired behaviors using treats, toys, or praise, and they ignore or redirect unwanted behaviors. Therefore, a positive trainer may ask a dog to sit. If the dog does not sit, the trainer may walk away or ignore the dog if she believes the dog understood the cue but chose not to comply. The trainer may then again ask the dog to sit and if the dog complies, then the dog will receive a reward or treat.

Force free trainers do not speak of dominance or alpha in the relationship. Instead, these trainers generally believe that a dog's refusal to follow the handler's requests often occur because the dog either does not fully understand what behavior they ought to perform, or the dog is acting out because of some kind of distraction, pre-existing fear, anxiety, or other stress such as a health problem. Positive reinforcement trainers contend that positive reinforcement training works to change any behavior if done correctly and often use examples of positive reinforcement working for many different types of animals and even humans.

"Whatever the training task, whether keeping a four-year-old quiet in public, housebreaking a puppy, coaching a team, or memorizing a poem, it will go faster, and better, and be more fun, if you know how to use reinforcement." Karen Pryor, Don't Shoot the Dog.

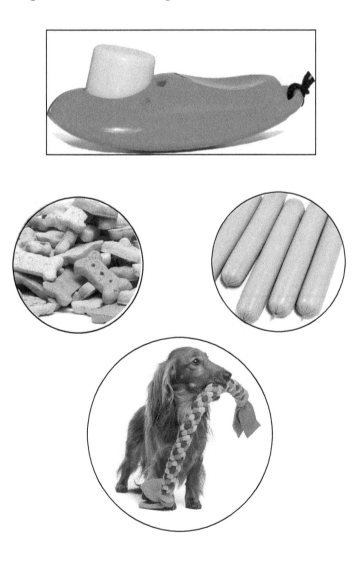

The Origins of Positive Reinforcement

B.F. Skinner is often regarded as the father of positive reinforcement. Skinner was an American psychologist, who in 1938 coined the term operant conditioning which essentially means changing of behavior through the addition or subtraction of things an animal likes or dislikes as a consequence of the behavior.[8] One aspect of operant conditioning is positive reinforcement which means a good consequence occurs after a behavior happens.[9] Skinner showed how positive reinforcement works by placing a hungry rat in his "Skinner Box." The box contained a lever on the side. When the rat moved around the box, it would accidentally knock the lever and a food pellet would drop into a container next to the lever. The rats quickly learned to trigger the lever. The consequence of receiving food if they pressed the lever ensured that they would repeat the action over and over.

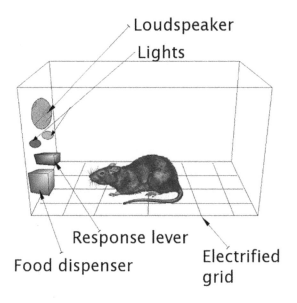

Loudspeaker

Lights

Response lever

Food dispenser

Electrified grid

Skinner also studied the impacts of adding pain or discomfort to change behavior. For example, he performed experiments using rats that received a light electric shock. The shock continued until the rat moved a lever, then the shock would stop. In this situation, the rats also generally learned to push the lever. However, this type of punishment may cause other problems. These problems include:

▷ Punishment tends to increase aggression.

▷ Punishment tends to create fear that can generalize to other behaviors.

▷ Punishment does not necessarily guide toward desired behavior. Punishment only tells you what not to do.[10]

Soon Skinner sought to use Operant Conditioning to teach other behaviors. In 1943, Skinner and two of his graduate students decided to see if they could teach a pigeon to bowl in a laboratory. They started by putting the pigeon and a wooden ball with an automatic feeder like his Skinner box. They initially wanted to trip the feeder when the pigeon swiped at the ball with its beak. But the pigeon did not swipe at the ball as they had hoped.

Skinner then decided to reinforce any interest in the ball. Therefore, when the pigeon even looked in that direction, he clicked the switch which fed the pigeon corn. With repetition, the pigeon soon learned to associate the ball with a reward. Skinner later wrote, "The result amazed us. In a few moments, the ball was caroming off the walls of the box as if the pigeon had been a champion squash player."[11]

Operant conditioning was soon refined with the use of clickers which are training tools that make a clicking sound. The sound is similar to the sound of the lever moving and the dropping of a treat in Skinner's box telling the animal that a reward is coming. Eventually, two of Skinner's graduate students—Marian Breland Bailey and her first husband, Keller Breland—founded *Animal Behavior Enterprises (ABE)* in 1947 whose mission was to demonstrate a better, scientific way of training animals in a humane manner using positive reinforcement.[12] The Brelands primarily used the new type of clicker training to train animals for commercials and in zoos.

Eventually, clicker training started also being used to train a wide variety of animals including marine mammals. One marine mammal trainer, Karen Pryor, eventually tried to bring the information regarding clicker training and operant conditioning to the general public. In 1984, she published a book *Don't Shoot the Dog* which became well known as one of the first books promoting the use of clicker training for the general public in dog training.

Times Are Changing—What We Have Learned

Since each of these theories of training originated in the early to mid 1900s, attitudes have changed in the world of behavior. In the area of human behavior, the physical punishment or correction mindset has been largely abandoned. Many studies have shown that when children are spanked, they are more likely to show aggression later and they are more likely to use violence to exert power over others (i.e. bullying and domestic violence).[13] As a result, the use of corporal punishment to teach and change behavior has been essentially abandoned in public schools and in our judicial system.

The cultural change of how we raise our children started a movement to study the way we train dogs and reexamine the theories underlying traditional, correction based training. Karen Pryor was one of the first trainers to put forth the idea that physical pain is not required for dog training. Behaviorists Dr. Karen Overall, Dr. Ian Dunbar and Dr. R. K. Anderson were also early pioneers of this process. These people realized that dogs are dogs and they will make mistakes—just as a human is only human—and therefore, they began to question the use of pain as a teaching technique. They saw that if we can more humanely teach animals, we all benefit from the result.

What makes these individuals different from the traditional trainers mentioned above is the vast amount of scientific data that supports their claims and shows that traditional training can cause more harm than good when training dogs. These studies show:

▷ Punishment can cause aggressive behavior and therefore puts individuals near a dog trained in this way at risk of being attacked.[14]

▷ If the punishment is not strong enough, the animal may develop a tolerance to the pain, so that the handler needs to escalate the intensity.[15]

▷ Using force causes a risk of permanent physical injury including:

   ▷ Electronic anti-bark collars can cause burn marks on dogs.

   ▷ Choke chains can damage the trachea, increase intraocular pressure in dogs thus potentially worsening or contributing to glaucoma in susceptible breeds, cause sudden collapse from non cardiogenic pulmonary edema (water in the lungs) due to temporary upper airway obstruction, and cause nerve damage.[16]

Additionally, scientists have looked at the long term psychological impacts of correction based training. To do these studies, scientists spend time observing dogs' body language looking for signs of pain and discomfort in the animals during training. This body language includes vocalizations from pain, tongue flicking, licking lips, and other postures that express fear. One such study researching the short and long-term behavioral impacts of using shock collars found:

▷ shocked dogs are more stressed than control dogs on the training grounds;

▷ shocked dogs are also more stressed than control dogs in the park;

▷ shocked dogs connect their handlers with getting shocks;

▷ shocked dogs may also connect orders given by their handlers with getting shocked.[17]

> *"The conclusions, therefore, are that being trained is stressful, that receiving shocks is a painful experience to dogs, and that the dogs evidently have learned that the presence of their owner (or his commands) announces reception of shocks, even outside of the normal training context. This suggests that the welfare of these shocked dogs is at stake, at least in the presence of their owner."[18] Matthijs B.H. Schilder and Joanne A.M. van der Borg*

Positive Reinforcement Training Is at Least as Effective, and Often Times More Effective than Traditional Training

On the other hand, positive reinforcement training provides a faster and more efficient training method. Take the experience of Guide Dogs for the Blind as an example. Guide Dogs had historically used traditional training methods for its service animals. Using traditional training methods, approximately 45 to 50 percent of the dogs entering the formal training process made guide dog status. After incorporation of positive reinforcement based training, the graduation rate increased. Now 60 to 85 percent graduate and are successfully paired with a blind partner.[19] Guide Dogs has noticed that they are producing dogs that are more enthusiastic, better thinkers, and problem solvers.

In response to studies and results like this, traditional trainers have suggested that the use of pain, such as in the use of shock collars, is justified because some behaviors require correction based methods for success and that the pain is not significant. Therefore, these methods provide long-term welfare benefits which off-set the pain and discomfort to the dog during training.[20]

The justifications I hear most often are, "If the use of the shock collar makes the dog listen so it does not run in the street and get hit by a car when chasing a cat, some amount of pain during training is worth it," or "Severe behavior issues are the number one reason that dogs end up at the pound, so using correction based training is actually saving dogs' lives." These statements certainly pull on our emotions, but they also assume that using positive reinforcement training will not work on hard behaviors such as prey drive (chasing animals) or other deeply ingrained behaviors. This is simply not true.

Take, for example, a study of 63 pet dogs that were assigned to trainers for problems related to recall around livestock.[21] The dogs were split into three groups and each group received two 15-minute training sessions per day for five days.

▷ Group A went to trainers approved by the Electronic Collar Manufacturers Association who used shock collars.[22] These trainers corrected the dogs with the shock collars, but also gave positive reinforcement such as food, play or praise for compliance.

▷ Group B went to the same trainers as Group A but without electronic collars. This group of dogs also was given positive reinforcement for compliance.

▷ Group C went to trainers using only positive reinforcement based techniques by members of the Association of Pet Dog Trainers, UK.

At the conclusion of the study, 92% of the dog owners reported improvements in their dogs' behavior with no significant difference in the response to training between the groups. No matter what method they employed, the dogs' behavior improved the same amount and this was in relation to a high prey drive behavior where traditional trainers often claim only correction techniques will work. But while the dogs' ability to learn to stop chasing livestock was the same, the observable stress between the different groups of dogs was far different.

Dogs trained with the shock collars showed significantly more signs of stress. They were more tense and interacted less with their environment, compared to the dogs trained using positive reinforcement based training. In some instances they yelped when shocked. This is true even though the trainers were hand selected by the shock collar manufacturers. They used the manufacturer recommendations for administering the lowest shock level possible and gave warning beeps with the collars before shocking. Ultimately the study concluded that there is no consistent benefit gained from shock collar training compared with positive reward based training. In other words, if both techniques are equally effective for controlling prey drive, there is no reason to use the methods that cause pain, stress, and other potential emotional problems.

In my experience, along with scientific evidence supporting these observations, I have seen many dogs trained by using a choke chain, pinch collar, or electric shock collar who show significant signs of stress when I start training with them. In some cases, the harsher training techniques caused the dog to turn on their human, which often led them to me in the first place. In most cases, these dogs only display this behavior when they are hurt by the shock collar while being trained and have never shown any other aggression to people. But the harsh training techniques often leave other long-standing problems with the dogs such as chronic fear, mistrust of people, and other emotional problems that I eventually have to address.

Why Are We Stuck in a Bad Tradition?

In stark contrast to the vast amount of science supporting positive reinforcement training as a pain-free and generally better method of training, traditional trainers can point to few if any studies conducted in the last 60 years that support the contention that pain is a necessary component of training. Much of their training philosophy leans on theories that are 60 to 100 years old. Yet they still resist doing things in a safer, more humane way.

Just think about how much the rest of the world has changed in the last 100 years. Because of advances in research, science, and education, our world has literally transformed the way we live. We use email or texting instead of writing a letter or calling. We have cell phones that can be used almost anywhere on the planet. Sending a human in space is no longer novel. Today, women are CEO's of companies and men are nurses. Men are stay-at-home dads who focus on communicating with their children rather than being dictators. Men and women are equal in marriages. Our dogs are becoming true family members and have jobs like helping the blind, helping people with PTSD, and sniffing out cancer. If we go back even farther and never challenged old beliefs, we would still think the world was flat.

Thank goodness, we have people in medicine, the automotive and computer world and NASA who don't think that way. We live in a world that is constantly changing. Often, our new discoveries improve our lives. There are now laws that protect children who have been physically abused.

While there is no law protecting dogs from being shocked repeatedly with electric collars in the United States, I expect that this will change as well. Nine countries in Europe and three Australian States have banned the use of shock collars in training. Prong collars and shock collars are banned in Quebec, Canada. One of the countries to ban shock collars is

Germany, home of the father of traditional training Colonel Most.

You may be asking why the shift has taken so long and why there are still trainers who use these outdated techniques. The answer is Colonel Most's dog training book was written over 100 years ago and spread through the world while much of the research on dog behavior has been conducted over the last twenty years. As mentioned in the introduction, the Semmelweis Reflex shows us that change is hard. People often live by the philosophy, *If it ain't broke, don't fix it.* Even with the research, we still have a dog training program on TV showing the old way to train. Sadly, we already know the old way has many negative side effects, but much of the general public and a lot of traditional trainers just don't know that yet.

Other trainers have adopted some of the force free techniques but often revert to corrections if they are not immediately successful. Some of these trainers call themselves balanced trainers (meaning they seek to reward good behavior and they punish unwanted behavior). In some cases, I have seen these trainers cause more harm than a trainer who purely uses punishment, because their praise or punishment is arbitrary or the behavior being praised or punished is not clear to the dog. These situations sadden me because I equate it to a domestic violence situation, and in many situations a dog's undying loyalty may mask the pain.

These types of dysfunctional interactions have been identified in abusive relationships with women who develop irrational emotional attachments to their abusers.[23] This phenomenon has been called *traumatic bonding*. It occurs as the result of ongoing cycles of abuse with intermittent positive experiences like the husband who beats his wife and then buys her flowers to get her back. Unfortunately, this pattern often leaves the women suffering from depression and low self-esteem. Isn't it possible that dogs can be affected the same way?

We Cannot Rely on Our Dogs to Tell Us Traditional Training Hurts

Lulu, a German Shepherd mix, came into my life a few years ago as a foster. She had been a watch dog for a local nursery. When I met Lulu, I could see her ribs under her thin, patchy fur. Under her dull coat, her skin was dry, thick, and grey like an elephant's. The owner of the nursery had taken her to the veterinarian because of her skin issues. She told him that he had to give her medication three times a day. Initially, he just asked me to board her for ten days to give her the medication.

After about five days, it was clear that her skin issues were much more serious and Lulu was going to need medication for much longer, possibly the rest of her life. The owner of the nursery told me he would need to euthanize her then because he could not commit to the long-term medication. Instead of euthanizing her, I agreed to foster her.

The day he came to bring me her things (a beat-up bed, poor quality food, and a filthy leash), he asked if he could see her to say good-bye. She was in my house at the time. When I agreed and told him she was in my house, he could not believe I let her live with us. When I brought Lulu out to say good-bye, she ran to him and licked his hand. He did not want to touch her because of her skin issues. It broke my heart to see that even after years of neglect, she still loved him unconditionally. Most dogs instinctively want our attention and affection. These dogs often seem to live by the idea that negative attention is better than no attention and are willing to instantly forgive mistreatment. This is not unlike children of abusive parents still seeking the attention and affections of those who hurt them. But despite the fact that abused dogs may still adore the person who has hurt them, this forgiveness is not a justification for continuing to cause physical or emotional pain. Dogs cannot speak for themselves. It is up to us to do the right thing for them.

"The dog tied up alone in the backyard howling for attention, the horse cribbing in its stall out of lack of companionship, the cat urinating all over the house because of unrelieved emotional stress—these animals are suffering. Their cries must not go unheeded." Franklin D. McMillan[24]

As we are learning more about how dogs learn and what is important to help them live balanced lives, the human-dog bond is getting increasingly more important. Dogs used to live in the back yard or they ran free through neighborhoods. In many homes, they are now treated as a child of the family. But since we now know that traditional training harms dogs, creates risks to handlers, and is not any more effective as a training technique, why continue to use unnecessary pain to teach?

There is only one logical conclusion: We must reject punishment and correction based training as valid dog training methods. Positive, force free training must become the only acceptable way to train. As humans, negativity and punishment surrounds us. Just watch the news on television. Wouldn't it be great to shift to more positive relationships in our world? If you think about it, this is not just about dog training. This is how we can teach anyone—cats, rabbits, dolphins, birds and humans. When we remove the violence, pain, and corporal punishment, everyone benefits.

Summary

> **Traditional training**—The basic philosophy of traditional trainers is to correct any unwanted behavior using a leash correction or "pop" and then praise the appropriate behavior. For example, a traditional trainer may ask a dog to sit. If the dog continues to stand (an unwanted behavior), the trainer will administer a correction or punishment using a leash pop. Leash corrections then will continue until the dog does the wanted behavior by sitting. The trainer then may praise the dog for sitting, but this does not always happen.

> **Alpha or dominance theory**—When a dog is resisting known commands, traditional trainers often tell their clients that the dog is challenging their dominance in the relationship and that the dog needs more discipline. They encourage handlers to become strong pack leaders or to become the "alpha" wolf of their "pack." This often means increasing the intensity and duration of the corrections until the dog submits. Some trainers go as far as

recommending giving little or no affection or rewards at all during this process to reinforce the handler's dominance over their dog.

▷ **Force free, positive reinforcement theory**—As opposed to using corrections, positive trainers seek to reinforce desired behaviors using treats, toys, or praise, and ignore or redirect unwanted behaviors. Therefore, a positive trainer may ask a dog to sit. If the dog does not sit, the trainer may walk away or ignore the dog if she believes the dog understood the cue but chose not to comply. The trainer may then again ask the dog to sit, and if the dog complies, then the dog will receive a reward or treat.

▷ **Studies have shown that:**

▷ **Traditional based training** can cause aggressive behavior and therefore puts individuals near the dog at risk of being attacked. If the punishment is not strong enough, the animal may develop a tolerance to the pain, so that the handler needs to escalate the intensity. Using force causes a risk of permanent physical injury.

▷ **Positive reinforcement—force free training** is more effective, and causes less pain and anxiety than traditional training. Positive reinforcement training is at least as effective as correction based training to change highly stimulating behaviors such as chasing livestock.

Two

How Dogs Think and Experience the World

Jelly, a sleek white American Bulldog, came to me as a foster years ago. She had rarely left her original home and had very little experience with the outside world. When she arrived at my house, she appeared terrified. When offered a crate, she leaped at the chance to hide. She stayed in that crate for almost three days straight, only coming out to urinate three or four times. She hardly touched the food and water we offered in the crate. We let her hide in a quiet room and talked to her every day.

On the third day, she decided to come out to investigate. Within a few more days, she began to play with me and my dogs. After she started to trust me, we started her socialization and training. She blossomed into a very happy and playful dog. I have had many cases where I allowed a foster dog to just observe our family and home life for a few days. Once they

37

seemed to understand our routine and feel safe, they became more willing to engage.

A Whole New World

The human world is a crazy place to live for a dog. In the city, there are cars, trucks, trains, people pushing to get to their destinations and so many smells. In the country, there are large pieces of equipment, animals that are big and small, and even more smells. Most dogs are born in a quiet room or house. They see maybe two to five people on a regular day. The only other animals they may see are the other pups and mom. The only smells they may experience are from that home.

Given the limited experiences of most puppies, humans have very high expectations for dogs when they bring them home. They assume that the dog should just understand that the human is planning to care for them, love them, and keep them safe. But dogs do not come pre-programmed for success. Depending on their genetics and past experiences, dogs (whether puppy or adult) will respond differently in new environments.

Imagine being taken from your home as an infant, child, or adult. You have no idea where you are going and no one from your home comes with you. You arrive at a new home and everything is different. In fact, this new home is a new country and it looks like a new planet. In this new country, you must live with a family. Since nothing from your past home is the same, you have no idea how to act. The people speak in a language that makes no sense to you. They feed you food you have never had before and you sleep in a room that is very scary.

Suddenly, everyone from the nearby houses comes to see you. The house gets very loud and everyone is touching you, talking to you, and at times yelling at you. You get so frightened that you feel the need to urinate, but you don't know where to go. The next thing you realize is you are urinating and someone, possibly a person from your new house, runs through the room screaming at you and throws you outside. All you want to do is to go home, but you have no idea where that is. You find a place to hide and stay there as long as you can.

Foster children and refugees often experience the fear and anxiety of being in a new home or country. Languages, customs, clothes, and rules are different from what they are

Puppy mill

used to. They make mistakes because they don't understand your expectations for them in their new world.

Imagine if you were from a puppy mill, a large-scale commercial dog breeding facility where profit is given priority over the well-being of the dogs. Many dogs born in puppy mills are born in the same cage that they spend their first few weeks of life in. These dogs must urinate and defecate where they sleep and eat. These puppies can have a much harder time transitioning into a new home.

The Similarities Between Humans and Dogs Cannot be Denied

Although it is easy to assume that dogs see the world very differently because they are a different species, if you study our anatomy, the differences are not as dramatic as you may think. It is not a surprise that our thigh bone (femur) looks the same, that our lungs and heart look the same, or that our inner ear anatomy looks the same. It is also not a surprise that our blood, kidneys, lungs, and heart all function in the same manner. But it may surprise you to know that our brains also have similar anatomy and physiology.

In recent years, scientists have begun to train dogs to lie still and have MRI imaging taken. The results indicate that dogs' brains react very similarly to our own in many respects. Like humans, dogs appear to possess brain systems devoted to making sense of vocal sounds, and are sensitive to their emotional content.[1] This indicates dogs can understand some of the words we are saying and the emotions that go along with them. These studies suggest that trainers who have preached against anthropomorphism (thinking that dogs have some thoughts and feelings similar to our own), may have been leading us astray. If our brains are similar, why wouldn't dogs have many of the same thoughts and emotions that we have?

The fact that dogs have similar thoughts makes sense considering the evolution of the relationship between dogs and humans. The domestication of dogs occurred tens of thousands of years ago. During that process, dogs gave up their independence and started relying on humans to survive. They left their pack social structure behind to live in our world which has led to some surprising results in their evolution.

For example, a study of 437 Beagles in Sweden tested the dogs' response after presenting them with a very difficult problem with a person they did not know in the room. The researchers found that without any prompting, most Beagles automatically went to the humans and sought assistance.[2] This is a response that does not occur in domestic wolves. The scientists believe that this propensity to look to humans is a genetic trait dogs developed during domestication. They have started to isolate two genomic regions that are linked with a canine need for human contact.

Even more astonishing, researchers from the University of Chicago and other international institutions have found that several groups of genes in humans and dogs have been evolving to become more similar over thousands of years.[3] The scientists in the study sequenced the genomes of four gray wolves from Russia and China, three Chinese street dogs, and three domesticated breeds which included a German Shepherd, a Belgian Malinois, and a Tibetan Mastiff. From these sequences, the scientists were able to isolate the genes associated with domestication and identify how long ago those genes developed. The research indicates domestication of dogs occurred approximately 32,000 years ago.

Next, the scientists compared the genes associated with domestication with the human genome. Remarkably, they found that some of the genes for things such as the transport of neurotransmitters like serotonin, cholesterol processing, and cancer have been evolving similarly in both humans and domestic dogs. It is amazing that two separate species could have their DNA start to interact in this way, but that is exactly what is happening. Dogs have developed so closely with humans, their genes and ours have actually evolved together, something called *convergent evolution*.

Consider, for example, a recent study in Japan which carried out a series of experiments that examined the impact of dogs interacting with their people. The study found that just looking into each other's eyes caused the release of oxytocin in both the dogs and humans. Oxytocin is a hormone associated with maternal bonding. Levels of oxytocin increase when you're close to someone you love.[4] This same reaction occurs when a mother and a child look into each other's eyes.

Dogs are also one of the only animals in the world that will instinctively watch where humans point or look for help when presented with a difficult problem. Our closest relative, chimpanzees, do not even do that.[5] All of these studies indicate that dogs have evolved to feel and see the world more as we do.

These scientific findings further indicate that dog training techniques based on alpha pack models and dominance are simply insupportable, because dogs are on an evolutionary path to think more like us than their distant relatives.

> "Learning from wolves to interact with pet dogs makes about as much sense as, 'I want to improve my parenting—let's see how the chimps do it.'" Ian Dunbar[6]

Additionally, dogs trying to dominate humans makes no sense considering how they evolved. Because of the many years of domestication, dogs do not survive well on their own in the wild. In fact, two of the only domesticated species that easily adapt back to the wild are cats and goats. Our dogs need us to feed them, give them shelter, water, and to generally care for them. It makes no sense that a dog would become the alpha or dominant member in the relationship, because threatening the one who takes care of you is not going to get you fed.

The wealth of scientific evidence has led to the American Veterinary Society of Animal Behavior (AVSAB—an organization of veterinary scientists and animal behavior researchers) to draft position statements denouncing dominance or pack theory as scientifically unsupportable.[7]

Within the position statement, AVSAB notes that dominance theory has many problems including:

> ▷ It will often lead to the use of physical punishment, which may suppress aggression without addressing the underlying cause. This causes an increased chance of being bitten.

> ▷ People who rely on dominance theory to train their pets may need to regularly threaten them with aggressive displays or repeatedly use physical force. Conversely, pets subjected to threats or force may not offer submissive behaviors. Instead, they may react with aggression, not because they are dominant but because the human threatening them makes them afraid.

> ▷ In the wild, even in dominant or submissive relationships that are well established, the relationship lasts only as long as the higher-ranking individual is strong enough

to retain this rank. Thus, high rank is short-lived in both human-animal and animal-animal relationships.

▷ The use of dominance theory to understand human-animal interactions leads to an antagonistic relationship between owners and their pets.

As science continues to provide evidence that dogs have evolved to think and act more like humans, difficult questions begin to arise regarding the ongoing use of fear and dominance based techniques in dog training. Namely, is dominance a valid theory of dog training and behavior modification or is it merely a justification to use otherwise inhumane training techniques? I believe that buying into a theory that dogs must be dominated to create obedience severely impairs our ability to see when we are hurting our animals and prevents us from empathizing with them.

"Dominance theory has shut off scientific research and has crept into medicine to the point where we think we can do things to animals, whereby we are asking them to submit. Dominance theory is insidious and has crept into everything we do with dogs and it's wrong. It has gotten in the way of modern science and I've just about had it. Every single thing we do with dogs hurts them because we don't see them as individuals or cognitive partners." Karen Overall, Pet Professional Guild Educational Summit, November 2016

Empathy for Our Dogs

As humans, we may often feel some stress when moving or staying in new places, but we have an advantage over dogs. We have verbal language (that other people know most of the time), so we can ask where the restroom is or verbalize a discomfort. Our brains also allow us to plan for the future and read signs to know where we are. A trained dog may have some advantage if they understand things like "sit," "down," "come," "go potty," but if the new humans they live with do not use the correct cues (or words the dog understands) they may as well know nothing. In addition, some of our human rules are arbitrary, inconsistent, and change from situation to situation. We are supposed to maintain quiet in one type of building (church or library) but we are loud at others (at bars or at a party). We should greet some people with a hug but with others we should shake their hands. These rules are confusing for humans, so how do we expect dogs to keep up?

Our inability to see things through a dog's perspective causes many people to commonly misinterpret dog behaviors as being aggressive or dominant. I once consulted with a family who thought their dog was becoming aggressive. The Cocker Spaniel, Joe, attacked another dog who came into his backyard with my client's neighbor. As we discussed the dog coming into Joe's backyard, I learned that the dog was known to Joe because she barked at him when they saw each other on walks. When the neighbor came into the backyard with the dog, Joe was startled which started the altercation. The other dog was not harmed. After we discussed the event, it was clear that Joe responded similarly to how a human would respond if an unfriendly neighbor snuck into the yard uninvited. People have shot other people for this exact crime.

Identifying Fight, Flight, and Freeze

Fear and stress are other significant issues that dogs must overcome in our world. Because I work with fearful and anxious dogs every day, I am no longer surprised that dogs are afraid of things that we as humans don't think are scary (especially if it is something they have never experienced before). But I find that a dog's fight, flight, or freeze response is one of the most commonly misinterpreted behaviors by my clients.

The fight, flight, or freeze response is a primal behavioral response seen in humans and many other animals. At its core, the response is about how we respond to extremely fearful situations and it is about survival. When faced with a life-threatening event, our primal instincts will tell us to react in one of three ways:

> ▷ Try to fight the threat,

> ▷ Run away from the threat; or

> ▷ Freeze and hope the threat goes away.

Lucy, a German Shepherd mix, was a very fearful dog and was too afraid to go on a walk when I first met her. After about a year of working with her, Lucy was able to walk around her neighborhood. During one training session, a large big rig truck came down the street while we were on a walk. Lucy had never seen a truck of this size before and immediately went into flight pulling on the leash frantically. Lucy was so scared that Amy (her human) and I had to sit on the ground with her and hold her. It took both of us to restrain her. I even had to cover her eyes until the truck passed. Lucy showed us her terror.

Fight, flight, freeze.

Fortunately, I had worked with Lucy enough to know that she generally goes to flight mode in fearful situations and I could tell she was afraid of the truck. But had I not been paying attention, I could have interpreted Lucy's leash pulling as her just misbehaving on the walk. Other dogs in the same situation may have gone into fight mode and might bark aggressively at the truck when it passed. Still other dogs may have gone into freeze and refused to move.

The problem is many people do not pay attention to their dog's emotional state and to what is going on around them. Therefore, when their dog suddenly sits down and won't move on a walk, they may attribute the dog's behavior to being stubborn when in reality the dog does not want to move because his fear is that he is getting too close to a busy road. Alternatively, a dog may be labeled by her handler as aggressive toward other dogs because she barks and lunges at other dogs on a walk, when in reality the dog is scared because she has not met many dogs in her lifetime.

Another important thing to understand about this response is the impact it has on our dog's ability to learn. If we are under stress, our brains focus on keeping us safe and cannot process new information very well, because our number one goal is to stay alive. During this situation, we are not equipped to learn.

> Haim Ginott, author of Between Parent and Child has a wonderful quote in this regard: "When a person is drowning, it is not a good time to teach him to swim."

For a dog, the ability to handle stress can range significantly depending on what she is experiencing and depending on the dog's individual ability to handle stress. When a dog is resting or calm, she may have no problem following cued behaviors. Then as the dog starts to become stressed, for example, when going on a walk in a new place, suddenly she may start having a hard time listening. At this point she is in the "stress threshold" or her "zone of tolerance." However, if the stress increases enough the dog will eventually go "over threshold." When a dog goes over threshold they go into survival mode, i.e., fight, flight or freeze.

Dog Stress Levels

Dog Stress Level

When a dog has gone over "threshold" attempting to train them at that moment will be useless. A dog that is over threshold is in "survival mode." Her sympathetic nervous system is activated which controls her body's response to the perceived threat. Adrenaline increases, heart rate increases, muscles contract and pupils dilate as her body reacts as if it were facing a life or death event. In these situations, it is better to just get the dog out of the fearful situation or to try to minimize its impact in these instances.

If a trainer fails to look at the dog as an individual who is fearful and views the dog's failure to obey as a dominance issue, the trainer may start punishing a fearful dog for misbehaving when the dog is actually scared. This is especially true if the trainer ignores the fact that some dogs "zone of tolerance" is larger than others. Therefore, some dogs will take far less stress before going "over threshold."

Dog Stress Levels

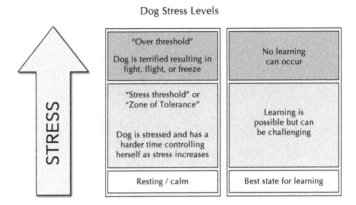

Punishing fear only compounds the fear. The dog may then intensify its attempts to run away or even go into fight mode and attack the handler. But if flight and fight do not work and the punishment continues, the dog will eventually freeze and shut down. In some cases, a dog may shut down so much that we call it *learned helplessness*—a sense of powerlessness arising from a traumatic event or persistent failure to succeed.

Unfortunately, I have seen this exact pattern repeated often on popular dog training TV shows. Dogs with underlying fear issues get punished for running or punished for fighting back. Eventually with enough punishment, the trainer induces the freeze response and the dog shuts down. the trainer then pronounces that the dog has reached a "calm submissive state." But the trainer hasn't done anything to make the events less scary or traumatic. In the traumatized state, the dog has not really learned anything except being helpless. Instead, the trainer has only put the dog in a psychological prison, like a battered wife who has given up trying to fight back. This pattern is dangerous for two reasons. First, people who use this technique run the risk of being bitten while punishing the dog. Second, there is no guarantee that the shutdown response will always prevent future aggression. Occasionally, battered wives do unexpectedly kill their husbands.

If we consider, even for a moment, what the dog's perspective is, I don't think training methods like this would be tolerated. Consider for example, being deathly afraid of snakes. One day you see a snake by the side of the road and try to run away. However, someone grabs you and forces you to get closer. In terror, you try to break free from the person's grasp but they are too strong. You next try to hit or kick your captor to get away, but every time you do, your attacker hits you back harder. Eventually, you lay on the ground motionless in terror praying that the snake does not bite you and hoping that your captor will let you go. This happens repeatedly over the next few days until whenever you see the snake and your captor, you immediately lay down desperately hoping they will leave you alone. Does this sound like a calm submissive state to you and shouldn't we be searching for a better way to address these issues?

Summary

▷ **Dogs are evolving to be more like us.** Through scientific studies we have learned that dogs process information similar to humans for things like understanding language and emotion. Other studies have shown that dogs' DNA is evolving to be more like humans.

▷ **Alpha or Dominance Theory**—These theories that dogs develop strict social hierarchy and need to be dominated to behave have been abandoned by the scientific community as unsupported and harmful.

▷ **Empathy and compassion**—Positive, force free training can help dogs adjust to the human world by helping us identify what is causing our dogs to have stress or fear.

▷ **The fight, flight, or freeze response** is a primal behavioral response seen in humans and many other animals. At its core, the response is about how we respond to extremely fearful situations and it is about survival. When faced with a life-threatening event, our primal instincts will tell us to react in one of three ways: Try to fight the threat; Run away from the threat; or Freeze and hope the threat goes.

▷ **Learning cannot occur when dogs are highly stressed**: *"When a person is drowning, it is not a good time to teach him to swim."*

Three

Making Life Easier for Our Dogs

Fortunately, there are many proven, low-stress techniques that can help dogs learn to cope with fearful and stressful events in their lives. The first step in assisting our dogs to adapt to our human world is taking steps to reduce or eliminate unnecessary fear and stress. Some of this prevention means working with the dogs while they are still puppies to help them better deal with new or stressful situations such as meeting other dogs or going new places.

Setting Puppies Up for Success

We have learned that puppies, like children, need to spend time learning to socialize with each other. Socializing puppies while they are young—under four months old—is very important for developing their social skills with other dogs

for the rest of their lives. Because dogs are almost adults by a year, we need to socialize them while they are very young and try to safely expose our dogs to as much of the outside world as possible. This is similar to the reasoning that children need to experience new things at a young age. Imagine a child growing up without ever leaving the home or being around other children and the potential social problems that could cause later on.

A puppy's prime socialization period is from about three to twelve weeks. During this period, puppies learn about the world including what objects, people, and environments are safe. During the socialization period, you want to avoid things that may lead to a significant fearful experience.

If your puppy does experience something scary, try to reintroduce the experience in a positive way. For example, if a puppy gets scared at the veterinary hospital, make sure you go back to the hospital for multiple fun, treatment-free visits. During the socialization period, it is important to avoid potentially scary or dangerous situations.

Steps You Can Take to Help Your Puppy During the Socialization Period Include

▷ Make sure all training is fun and avoid any type of punishment.

▷ Avoid going to dog parks or large daycare places. Wild, high energy dogs can scare younger puppies.

▷ Avoid forcing your puppy to do something he is afraid of. Instead, go slowly in these situations.

The average puppy may startle slightly when introduced to these new objects but will quickly overcome his fears; however, if your puppy seems overly shy, he may need extra socialization. In many cases, shy puppies benefit from consistent socialization for the first year. When socializing a shy puppy, you may need to go more slowly, but you will need to expose him to more things. It is critical that you make sure all new experiences are fun and stress free for your shy puppy.

Ideally, the breeder or rescuer will begin socializing the puppy before he goes to his new home, but this does not always happen. If you take your puppy home when he is eight weeks old, you only have four weeks left of his prime socialization period. This means that you must start socializing your new puppy immediately.

Unfortunately, many people do not start to socialize their puppy until they finish all of their vaccines, which generally does not occur until the puppy is sixteen weeks old or older. Some veterinarians still recommend that puppies not be taken out until after this time. Inside the behavior community, it is generally accepted that the benefits of properly socializing puppies outweigh the risks. Take reasonable precautions though.

Ways to Safely Socialize Your Puppy Before They Have Finished All of Their Vaccines

1. Have family and friends come to your house to play with your puppy.

2. Have your puppy play with healthy, friendly dogs that you know.

3. Enroll them in a puppy socialization class and be sure the class is held in a clean environment.

4. Take your puppy to the veterinary hospital for fun visits; have the staff give your puppy a treat.

5. Take your puppy in the car when you run errands. Be sure that the weather is appropriate—not too cold or too hot.

6. Take your puppy to the homes of family and friends.

7. Introduce your puppy to novel objects in your home (vacuum, washer/dryer, broom, boxes, skateboards, bikes, etc.).

8. Introduce your puppy to a variety of noises (alarms, banging pots/pans, blow dryers, buzzers, radio, TV, etc.).

In 2004, R. K. Anderson wrote a letter[1] explaining the importance of socialization in puppies. We still recognize this letter as valid and it is a position statement for AVSAB (American Veterinary Society of Veterinary Behavior). Sadly, R. K. Anderson passed away in 2012.

A Letter on Puppy Socialization from Dr. R. K. Anderson, DVM, Diplomat, American College of Veterinary Preventive Medicine and Diplomat of American College of Veterinary Behaviorists

---

To: My Colleagues in Veterinary Medicine:

Common questions I receive from puppy owners, dog trainers and veterinarians concern: 1) what is the most favorable age or period of time when puppies learn best? 2) what are the health implications of my advice that veterinarians and trainers should offer socialization programs for puppies starting at 8 to 9 weeks of age.

Puppies begin learning at birth and their brains appear to be particularly responsive to learning and retaining experiences that are encountered during the first 13 to 16 weeks after birth [Dr. Anderson is saying that the prime time for puppy socialization stops somewhere between 13 and 16 weeks, although more socialization occurs after that time]. This means that breeders, new puppy owners, veterinarians, trainers and behaviorists have a responsibility to assist in providing these learning/socialization experiences with other puppies/ dogs, with children/adults and with various environmental situation during this optimal period from birth to 16 weeks.

Many veterinarians are making this early socialization and learning program part of a total wellness plan for breeders and new owners of puppies during the first 16 weeks of a puppy's life — the first 7-8 weeks with the breeder and the next 8 weeks with the new owners. This socialization program should enroll puppies from 8 to 12 weeks of age as a key part of any preventive medicine program to improve the bond between pets and their people and keep dogs as valued members of the family for 12 to 18 years.

To take full advantage of this early special learning period, many veterinarians recommend that new owners take their puppies to puppy socialization classes, beginning at 8 to 9 weeks of age. At this age they should have (and can be required to have) received a minimum of their first series of vaccines for protection against infectious diseases. This provides the basis for increasing immunity by further repeated exposure to these antigens either through natural exposure in small doses or artificial exposure with vaccines during the next 8 to 12 weeks. In addition the owner and people offering puppy socialization should take precautions to have the environment and the participating puppies as free of natural exposure as possible by good hygiene and caring by careful instructors and owners.

Experience and epidemiological data support the relative safety and lack of transmission of disease in these puppy socialization classes over the past 10 years in many parts of the United States. In fact; the risk of a dog dying because of infection with distemper or parvo disease is far less than the much higher risk of a dog dying (euthanasia) because of a behavior problem. Many veterinarians are now offering new puppy owners puppy socialization classes in their hospitals or nearby training facilities in conjunction with trainers and behaviorists because they want socialization and training to be very important parts of a wellness plan for every puppy. We need to recognize that this special sensitive period for learning is the best opportunity we have to influence behavior for dogs and the most important and longest lasting part of a total wellness plan.

Are their risks? Yes. But 10 years of good experience and data, with few exceptions, offers veterinarians the opportunity to generally recommend early socialization and training classes, beginning when puppies are 8 to 9 weeks of age. However, we always follow a veterinarian's professional judgment in individual cases or situations, where special circumstances warrant further immunization for a special puppy before starting such classes. During any period of delay for puppy classes, owners should begin a program of socialization with children and adults, outside their family, to take advantage of this special period in a puppy's life.

- Robert K. Anderson DVM, Diplomat, American College of Veterinary Preventive Medicine and Diplomat of American College of Veterinary Behaviorists.

Once a puppy is past the socialization period, they may tend to startle and stay frightened about new places or things. It is much harder to help them overcome these fears, and they may remain fearful even as an adult dog. Using the training techniques described below can significantly help with these issues, but prevention by socialization is the best cure when possible.

Removal or Avoidance of Highly Stressful Triggers

For adult dogs, avoid or eliminate many highly stressful situations. For example, when I started fostering Jelly, I did not force her to leave her kennel initially. She was already stressed, and I knew that pushing her might only make matters worse. Therefore, I avoided pushing her to come out until I could tell that her stress level had subsided. Remember, you can't teach someone to swim when they are drowning.

In other cases, a specific trigger that causes a dog to become anxious or fearful may exist. A dog may be scared of skateboards for example. Initially, the easiest way to deal with a dog in this situation is to control the environment and avoid exposing your dog to skateboards. This is not a permanent solution, but until we are ready to address the situation through training (as discussed in later chapters), repeatedly exposing a dog to a scary object (a punishment without a desensitization plan) will only increase the dog's fear response. If this occurs, it will make subsequent training to address the problem more difficult.

When Stressful Situations Cannot Be Avoided, Seek to Lessen their Impact

Although humans cannot take away all of the stress of the new dog or puppy coming into their home, there are many things that can happen to make it a smoother transition. When a new dog arrives home and appears fearful, the house should be kept fairly quiet. This is not the time to have a huge party or invite multiple friends over to see the dog. It is also helpful to create places for the dog to go to sleep or to get away. A crate is a great option for this, but an area in a quiet room may be just as effective.

The Importance of Play to Enhance Learning

We can also assist our dogs by making sure they are receiving enough positive stimulation through play. Dogs and humans are two of the few species that continue to play into adulthood. Scientists have learned that playing with our dogs is an important factor in their mental health and learning. A study of 4,000 dogs at Bristol University, UK, has shown that just playing with our dogs greatly decreases the chances of them developing behavior problems such as anxiety, aggression, pulling on the lead, whining, and not coming when called.[2]

The positive effects of playing with our dogs also increases the ability of our dogs to learn new behaviors. A recent study using sixteen Labrador Retrievers looked at the impact of playing immediately after training.[3] A play group of eight dogs enjoyed a 30-minute session of intense playful activity consisting of a ten-minute walk, ten-minutes of off-lead play,

and then a final ten-minute walk while a second group had no play time.

The dogs who had received the play session after training were able to reproduce newly trained behaviors cues 40% faster than the dogs who rested after the training. Play appears to help stimulate learning and likely helps strengthen the bond with our dogs.

Play can come in many forms. Mental stimulation combined with exercise can keep your dog occupied by using food-dispensing toys. Many of these toys are available. Kong toys, Kibble Nibble Balls, and Buster Cubes are just a few options. These toys are equal to a Rubik's Cube or crossword puzzle for people. These toys are great because they help dogs learn to be self-entertained and can help some dogs learn to cope with being left alone. In addition to food toys, hiding toys and treats can provide your dog with mental and physical exercise.

Trying to Help Your Dog Communicate by Teaching Your Dog ESL

One of the best ways to start helping your dog deal with fearful or stressful situations is to begin communicating by teaching them English as a Second language (ESL). ESL was originally used in education as a method to help people from foreign countries to learn English. Because dogs communicate primarily through body language and humans primarily use verbal language, we must essentially teach dogs a new way to listen.

When we teach our dogs to understand verbal cues, we can begin to tell them how we want them to act in different situations. This eliminates the need to force them to behave. I have also found that when humans think about teaching their dog ESL, it forces us to spend more time focusing on how the dogs are learning and interpreting our actions. As a result, we automatically become more empathetic and more understanding.

How Do We Teach ESL to Dogs to Help With Stress?

Learn to Listen to Your Dog's Body Language

The first step to teach your dog ESL is to start to open lines of communication with your dog by reading dog body language.

Learning basic dog body language helps us understand how our dogs are reacting to our training. We can begin to see if the dog is perceiving the training session as rewarding or stressful. We can also begin to identify if there are things going on during training that are scaring the dog, making it hard to listen and learn.

Unfortunately, most humans have very little knowledge of what their dog is trying to say to them. If your dog will not do a behavior when at the park, but is perfect at home, consider a few things. The dog could be too distracted and can't think since there is so much going on. The dog may also be shy or afraid at the park, which is creating too much stress to perform the behavior. When a dog is afraid, humans often notice the bark or growl first (verbal) but before the bark or growl, the dog was very likely screaming, "I am scared," but he was using body language to express it.

In Chapter 5, we will go over how to read dogs' body language in greater detail, but being able to "listen" to what your dog is telling you is very important. Understanding if your dog is stressed, fearful, relaxed, or excited is key when teaching ESL. As mentioned above, if a dog is so scared that he is over threshold, no learning can take place, and the trainer may put herself and the dog in danger.

Learn to Teach Your Dog Using Positive Reinforcement

Start teaching with your dog using positive reinforcement. This will make your communication less stressful which will help your dog learn "English" faster. Given the stress involved with navigating a strange new world, it is not surprising that positive reinforcement has been shown to help dogs cope and learn faster compared to punishment-based training. Imagine the example of the dog being taken to a completely new place, scared and alone, and then adding harsh shocks or choke corrections. The stress and fear experienced by the dog would be far worse.

Using positive reinforcement can help with these situations as it can make your dog's learning less stressful, and it will also help create a stronger bond with you. Think back to a time you were learning a new language, algebra, or chemistry. These subjects are difficult for some people. If your teacher yelled at you, slapped your hand with a ruler, or did something else that made you uncomfortable anytime you were not perfect, how well would you learn? On the flip side, what if your teacher gave you a quarter for every correct answer and re-explained something that you got wrong? Which would you prefer?

Dogs learn just like people. They need repetition and consistency to learn quickly. They also learn best in low stress environments. We will cover the basics of how using cues works and how behaviors are learned in Chapter 6.

Use A Few Simple Cues to Help Your Dog Learn to Communicate

Positive reinforcement training is also self-reinforcing. Meaning, the more cued behaviors (behaviors that are triggered by a word, hand signal, or sound) that the dog knows, the easier it will be for a dog to repeat and learn new cued behavior. When we are teaching a person a new language we start by teaching a few simple words and then build from there. Dogs also need to start with simple behaviors before they can start to learn more complex behaviors.

Additionally, once a dog begins learning a few simple behaviors, this can help the dog to know how he should act in the human world and in new situations. We appreciate it when a friend tells us if a party will be formal or informal so we can dress appropriately and fit in. If we can give our dogs something they know how to do, it will help them fit in with new situations.

One of the first behaviors I like to teach a dog is "sit." "Sit" is a desired behavior in so many situations. My dogs tend to have a default—they sit if they are unsure what to do. "Sit" can be used to prevent running out a door, prevent jumping, prevent begging, and many other things.

Eye contact with your dog is another helpful behavior. By re-enforcing eye contact (which isn't actual eye contact, but I want the dog to at least look at me), I teach them to look at me so I can give them more information. My dog, Captain, is exceptional at this. One day, he was off leash while we were on a hike when he saw a buck for the first time. He was unsure what to do so he reflexively looked at me which allowed me to call him to me. He came running to me as the buck ran the other direction, and I rewarded him with a lot of love and delicious treats. The more trained behaviors a dog knows, the easier it is for us to communicate. We will go over in-depth how to teach dogs new cued behaviors using positive reinforcement in Chapter 6 and 7.

Make Sure the Cues You Are Giving to Your Dog Are Not Confusing

Teaching our dog simple cues can help them cope with new environments, but teaching our dogs cues also requires us to really consider what the dog is learning. For example, many people think that dogs know what "no" means, but in actuality this can involve confusion. As with kids, people often overuse the word "no" with their dogs to the point the dog has no idea what action he did wrong. If a dog is told "no" while counter surfing and eating a steak off the counter, he may not know which part you are yelling about—his front feet being up, being in the kitchen, eating the steak, or something else he is perceiving at the time.

If we are not clear with our dogs, we may cause them to become confused which can lead to more stress. For example, if in the above example, the dog believes that you yelled at him for being in the kitchen, he may try to avoid going in the kitchen. However, if he gets fed in the kitchen, his human may suddenly be confused as to why he becomes anxious and worried every time he eats.

Pay Attention to How the Dog Is Perceiving Your Cues to Make Sure They Are Not a Punishment

We also need to pay attention to how our dog is perceiving our cue, either as something positive or as a correction. For example, if the word "no" is used with some form of punishment intentionally or not, the word may take on a negative connotation for the dog and turn into a punishment correction. When a cue becomes associated with a punishment, we can unintentionally create generalized fear or stress about certain objects or behaviors.

This occurred during an agility class I was teaching. A dog, Muppet, who was normally quite efficient at the weave poles, made a small mistake. When teaching weave poles in agility, a dog is trained to snake down a line of poles like a slalom skier going down a mini course. When a dog enters the first gap in the poles, the dog should enter from the right side (the dog's left shoulder should touch the first pole). In this case, Muppet, accidentally entered wrong and touched the first pole with her right shoulder. Her handler said "no" in a firm tone, but when she said it, Muppet was already at the third pole.

When the handler tried to get Muppet to try again, the dog would not move and obviously did not want to try again. Although Muppet has never been physically punished, she is a particularly sensitive miniature poodle mix and she does not like being verbally scolded. Therefore, she viewed the incident as a punishment related to her doing the weave poles. She was particularly unhappy in this case because she did not know what she had done wrong. In her frustration, she initially shut down and flat out refused to do the weave polls again. We encouraged her to try again with multiple rewards and she was eventually successful, but you can imagine how much worse the incident would have been if she had received a painful shock or pop of a choke chain. After that incident, her handler never said "no" during agility training again because she knew she could inadvertently cause her dog to dislike agility.

I witnessed another situation when a dog was on a choke chain, and was inadvertently corrected by the handler. The dog was sitting nicely by the handler's feet when suddenly the handler inadvertently popped the leash. This startled the dog and he stood up. When he stood, it got the attention of the handler who then popped the leash again because the dog was standing. The dog became very confused and was not sure if he should sit or stand. Have you ever made a simple mistake and got reprimanded far more harshly than you deserved?

With force free, positive training your timing is also important as we are attempting to reward the dog right when they respond to your cue. However, if you make a mistake it is far less harmful. If you ask your dog to sit and you give them a treat before they actually sit, you can try again and wait for the behavior to complete, knowing that the dog will likely try again because he did not feel punished. Although this poorly timed reinforcement may slow training slightly as the dog could remain confused, it will not create unneeded stress or fear in the dog.

Learning Is Always Happening, so Pay Attention to Make Sure the Dog Is Not Learning Accidentally Cued Misbehaviors

One thing many people do not understand is that learning is always happening with their dogs whether they are intentionally teaching them or not. Skinner's theories of operant conditioning are basic descriptions of how animals learn behaviors. Dogs certainly learn behaviors we don't intentionally teach them all the time.

For example, Buster, my first Jack Russell Terrier mentioned in the introduction, loved to bark at the mailman. For a long time, I did not realize this because I worked when the mailman delivered our mail. However, when I was out on maternity leave, I notice that at about 10:00 every day, Buster ran through the house and barked wildly in the front window for about three minutes.

It seems that Buster had determined that a strange man in a uniform came to the door at that time of day and made some noise. Buster learned that when he barked, the strange man always left, which Buster perceived as a reward. Buster practiced this behavior for a long time and I could tell based on his body language that it was highly rewarding for him.

This is one of the reasons why paying attention to body language and the dog's environment is so important, because it allows us to see how our dogs are perceiving their world. We can then see if the dog sees our training as a rewarding experience which can help speed up learning new cued behaviors or as an unrewarding experience which will slow things down. If our dog is not experiencing the training or environment positively, we can make adjustments to make the training more rewarding.

This also allows us to discover the cause of behaviors that the dog has picked up that we did not intentionally cue, such as barking at the mailman. Once we understand what is triggering an already existing behavior, it permits us to start changing the underlying environment, cues, and rewards to change the behavior. This is true even if the underlying behavior is the result of strong emotions such as fear or high distraction, or chasing livestock as in the study mentioned in the last chapter. The process for changing previously learned behaviors is detailed in Chapter 8.

Summary

> Puppies should be socialized before they are four months old to help them become happy adults.

> Avoid fear-inducing triggers until you have time to train your dog to accept them.

> Playing with our dogs helps decrease behavior problems and enhances learning.

> Dogs will be less stressed and more successful if we can help them learn English as a Second Language (ESL).

> A mistimed correction (whether intentional or not) can cause stress and fear as opposed to a mistimed reward.

Four

Debunking Common Training Myths

Some dog training old wives' tales boggle my mind. Many years ago I worked with George, an elderly man who had cerebral palsy. Because he had very limited use of the left side of his body, he could not hold a leash with his left hand and his left leg dragged behind him when he walked. When I met George, he was struggling to work with his Jack Russell Terrier, Emily. Another trainer told George that he had to walk Emily on his left side. (Some trainers require dogs walk this way because walking on the left is a requirement in obedience and/or confirmation competitions). This was very difficult for George, and it led to extreme frustration when he tried to walk Emily. I immediately suggested that George begin to walk Emily on his right side instead. Not only was he stronger on his right side, he was also more confident. The relief George felt was clear on his face. George appreciated that I made training Emily easier and his walks with Emily were more enjoyable.

As we learn to understand the animals that we love and care for, we also need to understand the difference between the truth and old wives' tales. As a veterinary technician and dog trainer, I have heard many myths about dogs. The more we study and learn about dogs, the more we understand them and can see the mistakes in many of our myths.

All Dogs Must Go on Walks

A common myth among dog handlers is that all dogs must go on walks. A confident dog with little or no fears will often enjoy walks and even ask for them. Most dogs walked regularly as puppies will grow up to enjoy walks. However, dogs that are fearful or anxious or were not socialized as puppies may dread walks and find them extremely frightening.

If your dog shows fear of other dogs or people, then going on walks can become a punishment. If your dog pulls on leash and is showing signs of stressed body language as if they are running for safety, if your dog barks at people or dogs as they pass, or if your dog freezes and will not move while on a walk, then walks won't be the best option for exercise for your dog. If your dog does not enjoy walks, consider playing Frisbee or fetch in your backyard or playing games in your house.

Remember, exercise can come in many forms. If you have a large yard, you can play fetch. Additionally, you can use food-dispensing toys (Kong toys, Kibble Nibble Balls, Buster Cubes, etc.) to create games to give your dog physical and mental stimulation. However, if the problem is extreme, consider getting help from a professional who can help your dog overcome his fears.

Dogs Want to Go Everywhere with Us

People often assume that dogs should go everywhere we go. First, this is not always safe for the dog. Although some dogs may enjoy adventures with their human, there are some situations that are never appropriate. If the temperature is too hot or too cold, you should leave your dog at home. Because dogs mainly cool off by panting, they can get overheated very easily. Dogs should never be kept in a car when the outside temperature is hot. In addition, when the weather is hot outside, you should avoid taking dogs on walks or to street fairs when they will be on cement or asphalt. Because dogs do not wear shoes, the hot cement or asphalt can burn their feet.

As a veterinary technician, I helped treat two dogs that had been in the back of a pickup truck on a sweltering hot day. The pickup did not have a shell and the dogs' feet burned so badly from the metal that their pads blistered. The dogs had to go through months of bandage changes and their pads never completely healed.

Second, your dog may simply not enjoy where you are going. I often see miserable dogs at local street fairs. The dogs are forced to walk on the hot blacktop which sends many to take cover by dashing into any shade they come across. Other dogs are extremely stressed. For many dogs, walking amongst hundreds or thousands of people is overwhelming. Putting your pets through significant and unnecessary stress is a red flag for any trip.

It is important to remember that all of our pets are different. For example, if my family is traveling by car or RV, I know my dogs will love it. I also know that my cats would still rather stay home. Again, this is only for my family. I do know of cats and birds who travel quite well in a RV.

Dogs Hold a Grudge or Stay Mad at Us

People also think that dogs hold a grudge or get mad when they are left alone, because the dogs bark or are destructive after their people leave. More often than not, the dogs are actually experiencing anxiety when their people leave. Telltale signs of anxiety when left alone are that a dog will destroy something, urinate or defecate, or will become vocal only when the people leave.

Sadly, people often think that their dogs are holding a grudge when they are actually experiencing a panic attack when they are left alone. If you have a dog who does an undesired behavior when you are gone, you should get help from a professional who has worked with dogs that have anxiety when left alone. This type of behavior problem is challenging and may need medication from a veterinarian to be completely resolved.

When Dogs Bark and Lunge on Leash, They Are Being Protective

In my private training business, I work with a lot of dogs that bark and lunge at people or at other dogs when they are on a walk. Often the people think their dog is being protective of them. Although a small percent may be protecting their person, the majority of them are afraid and are purely concerned with protecting themselves, which puts them in fight mode.

Many times, these dogs exhibit multiple signs of anxiety and fear. If your dog is afraid, is he able to protect you? If you were afraid, would you be able to protect others? It usually takes a confident individual to protect others.

Once, I was home while our water heater was replaced. I had put our dogs in the backyard so they would not bark at the plumbers working in the garage. I had warned the plumber to tell me if he needed to go into the backyard. Unfortunately, the plumber did not heed my warning. I discovered him pinned against the back fence by my barking Jack Russell, Buster.

Many people may have thought Buster was protecting the house or me. However, when I went to get him, Buster stopped barking immediately when I picked him up. If he was trying to protect anyone other than himself, he probably would not have given up that easily. In reality, Buster got scared, and I saved him by picking him up, not the other way around.

Dogs Are Stubborn

A common thing I hear is that a dog is stubborn. I hear this when a person has a dog that refuses to move or appears to shut down when they are training them. However, questioning the people about what was going on when the dog became stubborn indicates something else is going on. According to the Merriam-Webster Dictionary, one definition of stubborn is *hard to convince, persuade, or move.* There are typically a few reasons I find that dogs get considered stubborn.

1. He is afraid so he freezes.

2. He becomes confused and is unsure what is expected.

3. The dog is not being rewarded very well for a behavior.

4. The cue has been poisoned. (A poisoned cue occurs when something that the dog perceives as negative happens after the dog performs the cued behavior. For example, the dog hears the word "come" and obediently responds. Instead of getting a treat or praise, he is put into the bathtub, which he does not like. Next time he hears "come," he may not respond because he fears it will lead to a bath).

As explained in the Chapter 2, dogs may freeze or shut down if they become overly afraid within the fight, flight, or freeze response. If a dog freezes because of fear, he may need to initially avoid the situation that led him to freeze until he gets slowly introduced to the new object.

For example, when dogs are brand new to agility, I often see them freeze when we introduce them to new equipment. The dog is just too scared to try. Because of this, I never force them on anything and I always start dogs on mini versions so they are not as scary. Many dogs are afraid to go through a tunnel, so I collapse it to make it as small as possible. After the tunnel is collapsed, I try to tempt them with a yummy treat. For more confident dogs, the treat is enough to encourage them to go through the tunnel. For more shy dogs, I may give them the treat for coming close, but eventually they carefully maneuver through the scary cave and come out the other side. Once they realize that it is safe, they go through happily.

Sometimes we confuse our dogs to the point that they tune us out. Often, we think we are being clear with our dogs, but if your dog appears confused, consider looking closer at your cues or training technique. You may ask for two things at once inadvertently, or your dog may not have mastered the behavior as well as you think. Commonly people will use a verbal cue or hand signal that closely sounds like or resembles another signal. In English terms, this would be like trying to figure out which form of a word to use—*two, to,* or *too*—when you are first learning, or if you should use *there* or *their*.

Sometimes, people will not reward their dogs enough for the behavior for which they are asking. When I am counseling a client about their dog's behavior, I often find that they are using boring treats but are asking for hard behaviors. If your boss asked you to do a hard project but did not give you a raise, would you do it? I like to explain to people that training treats are equivalent to a paycheck for your dog. We would all love our dogs to do things because they want to please us but sometimes that is not enough, particularly if we are asking them to do something hard or stressful. How many people do you obey because you want to please them? Would you obey even if you really did not want to or if you were afraid to do so?

There is a reason that reality shows such as Survivor have a prize of a million dollars. If the prize was a thousand dollars, many people would not leave their everyday life to do

such extreme activities. The high value of the reward moti-
vates individuals to do difficult things.

Another reason that a dog may appear stubborn is when
a cue is poisoned. We must always pay attention to how a
dog is perceiving our cues to make sure they are not becoming a punishment. A cue is poisoned if the dog is accidently
punished after he performs the correct behavior. I commonly
see this with recall. The person calls the dog, the dog comes
immediately, then the person puts the leash on (a cue that
"Your fun is over"). After a few times, the person is confused
why the dog will not come to them anymore.

*My favorite poisoned cue story is with a dog named Lady.
Lady was a beautiful chocolate-colored standard poodle. We
worked intensely with Lady's recall and she responded quite
well to the cue "Come," so I found it surprising when Lady's
humans told me she suddenly stopped coming. In fact, Lady
stop responding to "Come" and actually would run the other
way.*

*I soon learned why this was happening. Lady's people liked
to take her to the beach. They would let her off leash to play.
When it was time to leave, they would say "Come" to catch her
and take her home. Lady soon put together that "Come" really
meant "The fun is over." "Come" became so aversive (poisoned
cue) that we had to change her recall cue to "Here." To make
sure the word "Here" did not become associated with leaving, I
also had her humans call her using "here" multiple times when
they went to the beach to give her a treat. When she came, they
fed her and let her loose again. That way, the new cue stayed
positive and not associated with leaving.*

If I Use Food to Train My Dog, I Will Spoil Him and Always Have to Carry Food to Bribe Him

I commonly hear from people that they don't want to use treats to bribe their dog into behaving because it will spoil the dog and the handler will always have to carry treats. It is true that when using positive and force-free training, we usually use food as the paycheck to motivate our dog to want to learn. Food and treats are primarily used for teaching a new behavior. Once the behavior is learned well, the treats are decreased or eliminated.

For my dogs, I like them to understand the new behaviors and respond like a reflex before I start to remove the treats. For example, if they hear or see the cue for "sit," they respond instantly like we respond by braking for a red light when driving a car. At this point, my dogs will do just about any of the cues they have learned with or without treats. Once they know behaviors well, I occasionally give them rewards just to keep the behavior strong.

Of course, the same criticism is said of traditional training. If I use a painful leash pop or shock to get my dog to listen, I will continually have to inflict or threaten pain to get them to obey in the future.

When Dogs Wag Their Tails, They Are Happy

An extremely common misconception with dogs is that if their tails are wagging, they are happy. A tail wag just means that the dog is aroused. It is more important to see the manner in which the tail is wagging. If the tail appears tucked, the dog is experiencing stress. If the tail is erect and almost facing forward over the dog's back, he is overly assertive and may become aggressive.

Additionally, there are subtleties of how dogs wag their tails that we may not even perceive.[1] An Italian team of researchers investigated how study dogs reacted to other dogs wagging their tails. They showed 43 study dogs videos of other dogs whose tail wagging was more pronounced either to the left or the right. When study dogs observed other dogs wagging more towards the left, their heart rates increased and they became more anxious indicating they perceived some kind of threat. When the dogs' wagging was more to the right, the study dogs stayed relaxed. Of course, some dogs do not have a tail at all. In this case, it is important to look at more than one body part to determine the emotional state of the dog.

Any Dog Can Be a Service Dog

This is one of the most frustrating myths out there because it leads to unnecessary stress on the dog and disappointment for the human. First, I should explain the difference between a service dog and a therapy dog.

A service dog provides a lifesaving service to a human. *Guide Dogs for the Blind, Companion Animals for Independence,* and *Dogs for the Deaf* are a few service dog organizations. These dogs make it possible for the human to leave their homes safely, help indicate a seizure is going to occur, and can get the person to a safe place. They pick things up for people in wheel chairs, and they are the eyes or ears for a visually or hearing impaired person. In many cases, the human cannot live on their own without the dog. Service dogs are not a pet, they are a caregiver.

Therapy dogs, on the other hand, are well trained dogs that make people in hospitals, nursing homes, and veteran homes happier. With therapy dogs, there are also health benefits such as reduced blood pressure and decreased stress. Therapy dogs are not working dogs for the people with whom they live. They work by helping other people in the community. In short, service dogs are *nurses* and therapy dogs are *social volunteers*.

It is much more difficult for a dog to become a properly trained service dog than it is to become a therapy dog. Both require training but service dogs require much, much more. In most cases, a therapy dog must pass the American Kennel Club's Canine Good Citizen test (aka CGC). The CGC is a baby step to becoming a service dog. Before a service dog starts his journey, he is thoroughly socialized as a puppy, typically going everywhere with his trainer. As he gets older (roughly six months to one year) he begins intense training. In many situations, these dogs continue to go everywhere with their trainer and are being actively trained much of the time. Not only are these dogs learning how to behave in various environments, they are learning how to pick things up, how to indicate to a person that someone is at the door, and recognize a seizure before it happens. They even can differentiate between a doorbell and a phone ringing. They have many other skills that will eventually assist a person needing help.

There is more to being a service dog than just training. They also must have the right temperament and personality.

A service dog has to maintain calmness and comfort in any environment, they must not become anxious or fearful, and they must not get distracted easily. Although training can help with many of these, genetics also plays a key role. Even puppies that are born at service dog organizations with handpicked parents fail at becoming actual service dogs. On average, only about 50% of dogs bred specifically for service dog work actually become one.

I like to compare service dogs to Olympic athletes. To become one, you must have the right genetics, get the right coaching, and practice a lot. Like Olympic athletes, service dogs often miss out on many dog activities. Many Olympic athletes explain how they do not socialize, they don't have a lot of friends outside of their sport, and they are always training. Many Olympic athletes are homeschooled because they don't have time for school and training. It takes a special person to become an Olympic athlete, just as it takes a special dog to become a service dog.

Some Dogs Are Not Food Motivated

When I hear this from people, I often ask, "She does eat, doesn't she?" Of course, they always answer "yes." Some dogs may eat fast and others may eat slowly, but they all eat. Regardless of the speed at which they eat, most dogs have something they cannot resist and they must eat to survive.

There are many reasons that dogs are not food motivated. They may get fed too much at meal time so they are not hungry. They may have eaten right before a training session. Even I have to say no to a delicious chocolate cake if I am full. In many cases these dogs are actually fearful or anxious.

When in that state, the brain naturally decreases the appetite because it needs to focus on staying safe and alive in the moment. Another common reason is that the dog does not really like the food being offered. Although some dogs will eat *anything*, others have preferred tastes. I know humans in both categories.

If someone thinks that their dog is not food motivated, I go through the list of possible reasons why not, and 99% of the time we find the reason. In the rare case, if we don't discover the reason (or have not found the special food), training is reinforced with toys, petting, attention, and anything else the dog thoroughly enjoys.

A Hyper Dog Is a Happy Dog

Imagine a dog (often a Labrador, herding breed, or Golden Retriever) that is running around the house, the yard, or the park. The dog is having fun but is also oblivious to everyone and everything around. These dogs often do not have an off switch except for bedtime, when they pass out from exhaustion. We can see similar behaviors with people who suffer from severe Attention Deficit Hyperactivity Disorder (ADHD). Because I know people with ADHD, I know how hard it is for them to focus. They often unintentionally hurt others physically and emotionally, and find it hard to keep friends if they do not take medication. They also will tell me that they don't like the way they feel when they are hyperactive.

This is another situation when the body language of fear and anxiety are misunderstood. Panting, pacing, and hyper-vigilance are all signs that a dog is anxious. Because hyper dogs are not trembling and their tails are not tucked, their signs of anxiety are often missed.

The Neck Is the Strongest Part of a Dog's Body

I cannot believe that in the 21st century people still think this. I think it is a way to excuse the use of the pinch collar and choke chain, but I cannot be certain. It is not hard to understand that this is a myth if you contemplate that the first place any predator goes is to the neck of its prey.

Choke chains have been directly linked to the following medical conditions: ocular blood vessels, tracheal and esophageal damage, severely sprained necks, fainting, foreleg paralysis, laryngeal nerve paralysis, and hind leg ataxia.[2] Based on the number of injuries to the windpipe and neurological problems associated with the use of choke chains, it appears pretty clear that dogs' necks do not have any special resistance to injuries from choke chain or pinch collar corrections.

All Dogs Like to Meet Other Dogs When They Are on a Walk

This myth gets dogs and people in trouble every day. I often find that the people who believe this myth have never had a fearful dog, have never had a dog that is difficult to control, or they are friendly people who want to interact with strangers. However, dropping your dog's leash to let them greet strange dogs or having a dog that can pull you over to meet strangers can be dangerous.

First, a fearful dog may react badly if you let your dog approach. Believe it or not, there are many fearful or anxious

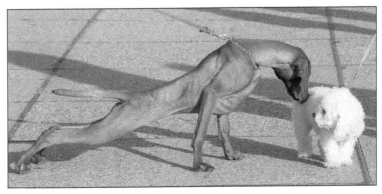

dogs out there, and as you read in Chapter 2, when fear or anxiety shows up, the result is either fight, flight, or freeze. If a dog experienced fight when afraid, he will often bark, growl, and lunge.

Second, an unsocialized dog may misinterpret your dog's intentions. Unsocialized dogs often do not understand how to greet a dog appropriately and do not read other dogs well. The unsocialized dog may interpret that a friendly dog is going to attack them and they may attack in response to a misunderstanding.

Finally, some dogs are enjoying their walk with their humans and may not want to be interrupted or have another dog in their personal space. We need to understand that dogs have personal space like humans. We don't like our personal space invaded and we don't like it if a stranger invades our child's personal space. We would never consider invading the personal space of an unknown child who was walking with her parents. We should all give the same courtesy to our dogs.

This is becoming such a big problem that an educational website called The Yellow Dog Project (www.

TheYellowDogProject.com) has been created. "The Yellow Dog Project is a global movement for parents of dogs that need space."

Summary

▷ Not every dog needs a walk.

▷ Dogs don't always enjoy going places with us.

▷ Dogs don't hold grudges.

▷ Dogs are not always protecting us if they are barking on leash.

▷ Dogs are not stubborn.

▷ Using food to train your dog will not spoil him and you will not always have to carry food at all times.

▷ A wagging tail does not always mean the dog is happy.

▷ Being a service dog takes special skills and personality.

▷ Dogs that do not seem food motivated may be fearful.

▷ Hyper dogs are often misunderstood and they are actually stressed.

▷ A dog's neck is not the strongest part of the body.

▷ Many dogs do not like to be greeted by other dogs on walks.

▷ www.TheYellowDogProject.com—an educational website for dogs that need space.

Five

Canine Communication

Our dogs are always trying to tell us something and it is our responsibility to listen. My dog, Captain, loves to play in the water, and he loves to fetch a toy that I throw into the water. One winter day, we went to the lake so he could swim. He excitedly waited for me to throw the toy into the water. I threw the toy and he eagerly jumped in to get it. After he retrieved the toy, I noticed that he was swimming parallel to the shore instead of swimming back to me. This was very unusual. Once on shore, he still would not bring the toy back to me so I could throw it again. I quickly realized that the water was too cold and Captain did not want to swim. Once I got the toy from Captain, I threw it on the shore instead of in the water. The relief on Captain's face was evident and he eagerly retrieved the toy and resumed playing fetch on the shore. Even though Captain did not use words, I was able to understand what he needed by knowing his normal behaviors and watching his body language.

The art of understanding your dog's body language is even more important than the techniques used to train your dog. Often when I interview clients who are angry, frustrated, or impatient with their dogs, I find that many of these feelings come from the person not understanding why their dog is acting out. Often dogs misbehave when frightened, stressed, afraid, or overwhelmed. Therefore, the frightened, overwhelmed puppy barks at the twenty kids running toward him. The puppy is often punished for being dominant or aggressive. In reality, that puppy is scared to death. In the moment, it would be equal to a lion chasing you. If you were tied down to something in that situation, you might yell too.

Katie came to me to help her with her dog, Carlie. Carlie was a medium-size mixed breed dog with a beautiful shiny, black long coat. Katie's main concerns were that Carlie pulled on leash and had attacked another dog. Katie adopted her about ten months before our appointment and they had worked with three or four other trainers before me. Every trainer they had worked with had used some type of aversive training technique to train Carlie.

The last technique (which was to give a hard jerk on the dog's neck with a pinch collar) had almost led to a bite for Katie. My client felt devastated that her new dog almost bit her when she was just trying to train her. During our first appointment, Carlie paced for over thirty minutes. She was clearly anxious and it was hard to watch.

To help her calm down, we put a Thundershirt on her. A Thundershirt is a type of compression suit that can help some dogs with stress. Within minutes, she laid down and slept for the rest of the appointment. In fact, she continued to wear the Thundershirt after the appointment and she slept for three days, something Katie had never seen her do.

During the first appointment, I explained that Carlie was showing signs of severe anxiety and I recommended that she stop walking her since it seemed that she was pulling because she was in flight every time she went on a walk. Sadly, some of Carlie's behavior was exacerbated because the trainers before me were punishing her for being anxious and afraid.

Learning and understanding dog body language is probably one of the most important things pet parents, groomers, veterinary staff, and anyone who works with dogs should know. Understanding dog body language helps us monitor if a dog is comfortable with a situation, or if he is anxious or afraid. For example, if a dog comes to a veterinary office and shows that he is scared, examining him in a room and physically restraining him by putting a muzzle on to give him vaccinations can create more extreme anxiety or fear. This can lead to aggressive behaviors and fight mode. The next time the dog comes to the office, he could be even more scared. However, if you identify the fear early, there are many training techniques (like desensitization and counter conditioning, discussed later in the book) or even medications that could be administered that would help the dog to make the veterinary visit a more positive experience.

Some dog body language mimics humans' body language as seen below.

If you like this poster it is available to download for free at https://trulyforcefree.com/product/body-language-poster-dog-8x10/

Some behaviors are unique to dogs. When dogs shake their body as if they are wet, when they pant excessively even though it is not hot, when dogs sniff excessively or shut down, they are usually experiencing stress.

When determining the emotional status of a dog, it is important to observe the entire body. Sometimes the face may seem relaxed, but the dog's tail is tucked tightly under the dog's body indicating anxiety or fear. He may act hyper-vigilant but his tail is wagging. Understanding a dog's body language can make training safer and easier since you will understand the emotional state of the dog.

Below Are Examples of Different Indications of Stress in Dogs

Panting, when it is not hot or they have not been exercising.

Licking Lips when not eating.

Hyperawareness. Looking around intently and can't be interrupted. Loss of Appetite. Won't eat even the highest value treat.

Ear Back. Ears pinned back tightly against dog's head.

Tail Tucked. Tail loosely or tightly tucked, but much lower than normal. You may even notice that the rear end is hunched slightly.

Whale Eye. Dog's eyes are looking so far to one side you can see the whites of their eyes.

Yawn. Full yawn when dog is not sleepy.

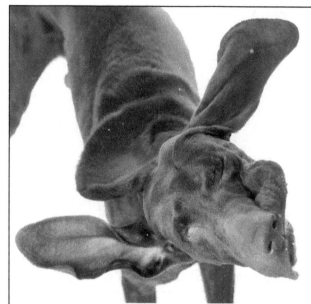

Full Body Shake. Like dog is wet when he is not.

Sniffing. Excessive sniffing when there is
nothing exciting to smell.

Snap. Dog will snap in the air with no intention of making contact, hoping it will make threat go away.

Unresponsive. Unable to respond to behaviors he knows well.

Behaviors that mean "Please stop what you are doing, I am very uncomfortable, scared or anxious."

Cower. Dog lowers body as if he is trying to melt into the floor and disappear.

Hard Stare. Dog stares at you so he knows where you are, hoping you will move away.

Growl. Will usually start low but will get louder if the threat continues.

Bite. Any dog pushed to his limit will bite in order to make a threat go away.

The time it takes to get to the bite is dependent on the dog's level of fear and the individual situation. The degree of the bite is often determined by how often the dog is forced to protect himself. A dog who has a fearful personality or a dog who has had to protect himself often may have a more serious bite.

When dogs are nervous or scared, they will show at least a few of the behaviors above. Dogs that naturally go into fight first may bark and lunge faster than a dog who naturally goes in to flight or freeze as a first defense. A dog who prefers flight may try to run away after exhibiting only a few of the above behaviors. A dog who naturally freezes in fear may display all of the behaviors. Every dog is unique, just as every human is, so no two will react exactly the same, even within the same breed. It is important to know your own dog's personality and limits so you can help keep him safe and so you can help him succeed. Understanding what dogs are telling us can help us be better dog parents and dog professionals.

Another important thing to remember is that correcting a dog for showing these signs of fear or anxiety will not eliminate the fear and can be dangerous. More often than not, dogs clearly express their discomfort before they bite. However, if a dog is punished for lip curling, growling, or snapping (humans will commonly hit dogs on their nose or scold them when they growl), we run the risk of getting rid of the dog's warning signals. As a result, the dog may skip giving a warning and go straight to a bite if pushed too far.

It is not uncommon for people (especially children) to be bitten when they are hugging a dog. It amazes me how many people try to hug a dog they do not know. Would you want a total stranger hugging you? I know people who don't even want friends or a loved one to hug them. I often wonder why it is that humans instantly hug dogs. It is something we need to stop. If we did, there would be far fewer dog bites.

Understanding Behavior Helps Decrease the Risk of Dog Bites

Beyond understanding body language of dogs, it is important to understand and respect the personality of each dog individually. Just like people, every dog will respond slightly differently to every situation. They will respond due to their genetics, their history, their socialization, and their experiences. Like people, some dogs are more introverted while others are more extroverted. Some dogs are calm and others are active. Some dogs are thoughtful and others are compulsive. If you want to learn more about your dog's personality and cognition, Brian Hare at Duke University has created a test called *Dognition* so you can understand how your dog learns and experiences the world.[1]

Once we accept that all of our dogs are individuals and, when we are knowledgeable about how they communicate, we can show more empathy and compassion towards them. Empathy and compassion lead to better relationships, it makes us better teachers, and there is more love and trust. Besides, the world can always use more empathy and compassion.

Summary

▷ Learning dog body language is extremely important to keep our dogs happy and safe.

▷ It is important to observe the dog's entire body when reading body language.

▷ Recognizing signs of fear and anxiety will help reduce biting incidents.

▷ Understanding dog body language leads to more empathy and compassion which creates better relationships with our dogs.

Six

The ABCs of
Dog Training

Learning can happen on purpose by being taught or with natu-
ral repetition. Years ago, I had a Flat Coat Retriever, Sadi, who
would occasionally react and attack my Jack Russell Terrier,
Buster. After a lot of observation, we noticed that Sadi's body
would tighten just before she would lunge at Buster. When we
noticed that she was getting tight, we would redirect her to her
kennel that was in the living room. Because Sadi loved her ken-
nel, and going into it when asked was almost a reflex to her,
she would go in immediately, saving Buster from being pinned
on the ground. Eventually, we started to notice that when Sadi
would begin to get tight, she made the choice to go into her ken-
nel on her own. The tightening of her body had become her cue
to go into the kennel. This reinforced Sadi because she loved her
kennel and because of the treats and praise we rained on her.

When we look closely at the act of training or changing the behavior of an animal, the process is actually quite simple. First, we must realize what is cueing or triggering a behavior to happen and recognize what is reinforcing the behavior so it is repeated. Second, we use tools to train or change the behavior as we see fit. However, just because something is simple does not mean it is easy.

To understand how behaviors become learned or why they occur, we must understand the **ABCs** of behavior.

Antecedent

A stands for **antecedent**. The antecedent is the cue that signals the behavior to occur. So what is a cue? In traditional training, a cue is called a command. Force free trainers avoid using the word command because it is a very dominating word. I want my dogs to participate in a cued behavior because we have a good relationship rather than a dictatorial one.

I also find that using the word *command* is misleading, because the cues that dogs react to are far broader than the oral requests that we give them. A cue can more easily be described as a *trigger* that can signal a behavior to occur. Cues are not limited to dogs. All animals respond to cues, including you! What do you respond better to—a request or a command?

If you train your dog to do a specific behavior and your relationship with your dog is good, most dogs will respond happily to a cue. If one of my dogs does not respond to a cue that they know and understand well, I look for a reason. If I cue my smooth coat Jack Russell Terrier, Scout, to lie down on a cold surface, she may not do it or respond slowly. Once I realize why she is not responding, I understand and realize I would not want to lie on a cold floor either.

I was working with a dog on an A-frame (a piece of agility equipment that looks like the triangle roof). She went on the A-frame once then refused to go on it again. Because it was usually one of her favorite obstacles, I knew something was wrong. After investigating, I figured out that the A-frame was very hot since it was in the sun and it had hurt her feet. I was able to cool it off with water and she tried again. After she realized it was safe again, I chose to practice something else that was not affected by the weather.

As humans, we interact with a variety of cues every day. When driving a car, a green light cues us to go, while a red light cues us to stop. We also have social cues. If a person stretches out their right hand, we meet their hand halfway with our right hand to shake. When a performer on stage finishes their performance and bows, we applaud. When the phone rings, we pick it up and say, "Hello." Cues are everywhere in our lives, but often we don't recognize them unless we begin looking for them.

Just like humans, dogs experience cues all of the time. When you pick up the leash, it cues your dog that it is time for a walk. Picking up your keys can be a cue to your dog that you are leaving. Many dogs even notice the difference between work shoes and walking shoes.

When training dogs, we are usually aware of the cues we intend to teach like using the word "sit" to get your dog to sit down, or when we point to the ground to teach a dog to lie down. When training dogs, we typically use words or hand signals when we consciously choose our cues.

What happens when we unconsciously or inadvertently teach a cue? One common example I see of this relates to people teaching dogs "come." A person will call their dog by saying "come" but may also lean forward every time they call their dog. The person may think the cue to come is the word "come," but the dog actually understands that he should come only when the person leans forward.

This can lead to confusion. The dog may unexpectedly come to the handler when the person leans forward doing something else. Alternatively, the handler may occasionally fail to lean forward while saying "come" and think their dog was ignoring them or being stubborn, when in reality the dog does not recognize the word. As a general rule, most dogs will learn hand signals (a body language cue) before they understand verbal cues.

The hardest cues to identify are those that are completely unintentional and can be very difficult to spot. For example, my Jack Russell, Scout, became afraid when the fire alarm sounded after my husband burned dinner a few nights in a row. Although we were aware that Scout did not like the fire alarm going off, we did not understand that Scout had developed an association between the oven and loud scary noises. The next time my husband turned on the oven, Scout ran out of the kitchen. At first my husband had no idea why Scout ran out of the room. The smoke detector never went off. Scout learned that when my husband turned on the oven (the cue) she would run and hide in our bedroom in anticipation of the smoke alarm.

Behavior

B stands for the **behavior** itself or what the animal is doing. Sometimes these behaviors are taught deliberately, like "sit," "down," or "come" for a dog. A horse is purposely taught to walk, trot, and halt, just as humans learn to push the gas pedal to speed up and press on the break to stop.

Just like the cues, many behaviors are learned unintentionally through experience. As humans, we learn behaviors inadvertently all the time. If a person gets food poisoning after eating a certain food, he or she may avoid that food forever. We also can learn important things inadvertently, such as being careful using a hot stove top if we were burned before.

Your dogs can learn inadvertent behaviors as well. If you only take your dog or cat to the veterinarian when they are hurt or to get a vaccination, they may become fearful of the veterinary hospital. Every living being is experiencing a behavior (and sometimes multiple behaviors) every minute of the day.

Consequence

C stands for **consequence**. The consequence is very important because it determines whether the behavior will increase in frequency or decrease. When the consequence is reinforcing or considered positive by the dog, the behavior will increase in frequency. When the consequence is considered negative or punishing by the dog, the behavior will decrease in frequency.

When we are actively training an animal, we often give some type of desired food to reinforce the behavior. This is what everyone knows as positive reinforcement. By giving the dog something pleasant, it is more likely they will perform the behavior again in order to receive something pleasant again. Eventually, the behavior will be linked to the positive consequence and your dog will happily do the behavior even when the consequence is not present.

This is basically the model humans live by when they go to work. People perform specific jobs or behaviors, and they receive money as the reinforcement. It is fairly well understood that when a human or animal receives something they like or want for doing a behavior, they are more likely to repeat the behavior. Humans do not always need money as a reinforcement. Our world is filled with many wonderful volunteers that never receive a penny, but the feeling they get from volunteering is extremely reinforcing.

However, undesired consequences can cause the behavior to decrease. If a human gets a speeding ticket on the freeway, he is less likely to speed in the future. If a person goes to a restaurant and the meal or service is terrible, he may never go to that restaurant again. As you can see, abuse or physical pain does not have to occur to stop a behavior. The consequence simply must be undesired.

The value of the reinforcement is important to consider and it is completely determined by the dog. Some dogs will happily do anything for a piece of kibble, but other dogs may need hot dogs or cheese. Dogs have preferences just like people. Some people love peanut butter cookies, but to other people they are disgusting. When you are training your dog, you want to make sure that you are using a reinforcement that he or she likes. I like to have a variety of treats when I am working with dogs. I have low value treats that I give for behaviors they know well or that are very easy, and high value treats for harder or newer behaviors I am teaching. Low value treats are usually things like kibble or another biscuit-like treat. High value treats are often hot dogs, peanut butter, or cheese. Remember, it depends on what your dog likes. Some dogs love their kibble in which case kibble may be high value for that dog.

When training dogs, we typically use treats because dogs love them and they are fairly easy to carry and distribute. Dogs can also find toys to be highly reinforcing, but they can be harder to carry and the playtime can slow down the number of repetitions you can do during a training session. Dogs may also find praise to be reinforcing, but it may not be a high enough reinforcement for a difficult behavior.

High Value Treats	Low Value Treats
Hot dogs	Kibble
Peanut butter	Dry dog treats
Cheese	Cheerios or other cereal
Soft dog treats	Crackers
Cooked chicken	Carrots or other veggies
Canned baby food	Bread
Cream cheese	Strawberries and other fruit

It is important to realize your dog's choice to respond or not respond to your cue is completely dependent on the consequence. If the consequence is liked by the dog, the behavior will more likely be repeated. We know dogs do respond when the threat of punishment is a possibility, but they are responding to fear. Do you want your dog to be afraid?

Tools That Will Help You Teach Your Dog

I will not go into great detail about all of the different techniques that train using positive, force free techniques because there are many good books, videos, and websites that can help with that. You can also find free information and videos about how to use these techniques on my website Truly Force Free Animal Training (trulyforcefree.com). Here is an overview of some techniques that you could start using right away.

Luring

With luring, a treat is placed in front of the dog's nose and you move the treat in a way so that the dog must change his body position (or perform a specific behavior) in order to get the treat. Luring is commonly used to teach "sit" or "down" by raising or lowering the treat so the dog moves into the desired position. If you want the dog to go onto a dog bed you can lure them by tossing a treat onto the bed or using a treat in your hand to coax the dog to step on the bed.

Clicker/Marker Training

When using a clicker, the dog learns that when he hears the click he has done the desired behavior and he will get a treat for his efforts. The clicker marks the correct behavior. Sometimes people use other markers such as their voice and say "yes" or "good" or use a whistle. I generally do not recommend people use their voice as markers when starting out. Since we talk to our dogs all of the time, we may use similar words which could confuse the dog, especially in stressful situations. How often do you say "good boy/girl" or "yes—that's it!" when you are happy with your dog? These things are okay to say, but they may not be effectively "marking" the specific behavior. Because the clicker has a unique sound, it may be more easily recognized in high-distraction situations, and it is more clear to your dog that they have done the desired behavior.

Capturing

A clicker is often used when a trainer is trying to capture a behavior but it is not required. To capture a behavior means that you reinforce a behavior your dog naturally repeats and then it is put on cue. If your dog lies on his dog bed every night, you could give him a treat every time he is lying on the bed. Once he realizes what you are reinforcing, you may notice him going to his bed more frequently or looking at you and then going to the bed. You can add a cue when he is moving to the bed or when he is on the bed. The more you practice, the faster he will learn it as a cued behavior.

Shaping

The word shaping is a term for building a behavior by using a series of small steps to achieve it. This process was described in Chapter 1 when Skinner taught the pigeon to bowl. As you may recall, Skinner put a pigeon in a box with a ball and he wanted the pigeon to push the ball. At first the pigeon was not even touching the ball. Skinner then began to reinforce any interest in the ball. When the pigeon even looked in that direction, he clicked the switch which fed the pigeon corn. By reinforcing interest in the ball, Skinner soon had the pigeon getting closer and closer to the ball until the bird began hitting the ball with its beak.

Now that we have an understanding of what the ABCs are and some basic training techniques, you can use them when trying to train or change a behavior.

Using the ABCs

The ABCs can be used to teach a new behavior or when trying to change an existing behavior. Teaching a new behavior is often easier, because we are only teaching one thing. Changing an existing behavior often involves eliminating the old behavior and teaching a new behavior to replace the old one. For example, if you want to teach your dog to sit when you say "sit," then you must only worry about your dog understanding the word "sit" as a cue to sit down. However, if you are attempting to change a behavior such as having your dog sit when you walk in the door at the end of the day instead of jumping up on you, then there are two behaviors at issue. The dog needs to learn to stop jumping and to sit instead when you get home.

Because of these differences, I discuss using the "I-ROAR" training technique as a simplified way of using the ABCs to teach a new behavior in Chapter 7. In Chapter 8, I explain techniques to change existing behaviors. However, I think it is helpful to walk through teaching a simple cued behavior such as "sit" to get a better understanding how the ABCs work.

Teaching "Sit" using the ABCs

1. First, get your dog to perform the behavior (sitting) using luring, clicking, capturing, or shaping without using an active cue. This means you must have your dog repeat the behavior you want without saying "sit" or using any other cue you plan to use. For example, a common way to teach a dog to sit is by luring the dog into the sit position. To do this you hold a treat in front of a dog's nose and slowly raise it up. The dog naturally lifts his chin so he can continue to smell the treat with the hopes that he will get to eat it. In most cases this will cause the dog's rear end to move towards the floor. When the dog's rear end touches the floor, he can eat the treat. This by itself uses all the elements of the ABCs. The **antecedent** or cue to sit becomes lifting of the treat above the dog's head. The **behavior** is sitting. The **consequence** is getting a treat. If practiced enough, the dog will be reliably sitting when the trainer holds the treat over the dog's head.

2. Second, you add a cue that you intend to use to signal the behavior. Since most people want a cue that is easier than holding a treat over the dog's head, this would be the time to add a different antecedent or cue. To add the new cue, you would offer the new cue as your dog

performs the behavior . In this instance, you could say "sit" as the dog's rear end touches the ground. This would be considered a verbal cue. Initially, you may still need to lure your dog a few times until he understands that the word "sit" means rear end touching the ground. Once he understands the verbal cue "sit", luring with the treat (the old cue) can be phased out. Now the new antecedent or cue is the word "sit." The behavior is still sitting and the consequence is still a treat.

3. Once the dog sits when he is cued to sit, the trainer can gradually reduce the amount of reinforcement and/or reduce the value of the reinforcement. The trainer may decide to only give a treat after two or three successful behaviors or may offer verbal praise or a scratch for doing the behavior. Even when behaviors become mastered, it is always a good idea to surprise your dog with a high-value reward for doing an easy behavior. After all, we all like to get surprises or bonuses once in a while, don't we?

Sometimes our dogs can also train us using the ABCs. My dog, Captain, likes to jump on my bed and will roll on me as a way to play or sometimes to try to get me out of bed so he can have breakfast. Of course, this makes me laugh, which consequently rewards him. Sometimes when he does this, I will snuggle him and scratch his belly which he likes. However, Captain only likes to snuggle for a little bit. When he is ready to get up *he will begin to wiggle. If I am not ready to stop snuggling, I will continue to hold him. One time he sneezed when he was trying to escape, and I let go and laughed. Because Captain is very smart, it only took one time. Now, anytime he has enough snuggle time, he will begin to sneeze (the **antecedent**) instead of wiggle, which causes me to let him go (the **behavior**) which keeps me from getting sneezed on (the **consequence**).*

Another more common example is when dogs learn to sit when their handler stops at a curb. Typically, the dog is first trained to sit in various situations and environments. For the next step, the dog will be on a walk and the person walking him will say "sit" to cue the dog to sit and the dog will get a treat. If the person walking the dog cues the dog to sit at every curb, the dog will soon learn that the curb is also a cue to sit. With time, the verbal cue "sit" is dropped and the dog will sit at every curb.

Summary

> **Antecedent** is the cue or signal that starts the desired behavior.

> **Behavior** is the action taken.

> **Consequence** is what increases or decrease the chance of the behavior being repeated.

> When dogs receive positive consequences after a behavior, they are more likely to happily choose to do the behavior again. Dogs can learn cued behaviors when

they are punished, but they are choosing to perform the behavior due to fear of being punished. Which do you prefer, a happy or a fearful dog?

▷ Learning happens on purpose as well as unintentionally.

▷ The value of the reinforcement is important and high value treats should be used when teaching a challenging behavior.

Seven

Positive Reinforcement in Action

My epiphany that positive training was more effective than traditional training happened when I was training my Jack Russell Terrier, Buster. He was about four months old, and I was trying to teach him to lie down. With traditional training, I was taught was to pull down on the choke chain until he laid down, then release the pressure. However, Buster had different ideas and resisted the pressure. Needless to say, we were both frustrated. Out of desperation, I went to the refrigerator and got out some cheddar cheese. Within a few attempts at luring him into a down, he was lying down. After that, I threw away the choke chain and began to study positive reinforcement techniques.

Dogs learn best when things are black and white. In fact, it is easier for anyone to learn when the rules are clear. When we are training a dog, it is important that they know when they are correct and when they need to try again. When using a clicker or other type of behavior marker, it allows our dog to know exactly what behavior earned the reward. This is the same training technique used for dolphins and other marine mammals. The animals learn that the click or whistle means that they did the correct behavior and they will get a reward for it. We often use treats as a reward but rewards are anything that the dog really likes. It is important to note that the value of the reward (how much the dog likes it) should always be considered. If a behavior is hard, a higher value reward should be given.

As smart as we humans are, we often make things more difficult than necessary. This is true in the field of dog training. Look at any pet store, pet website, and the thousands of dog training books and equipment available, and you will see many techniques. In reality, we do not need all the fancy tools to teach our dogs. We just need to understand why they do what they do and how they learn most effectively.

Whether you realize it or not, you have a relationship with your dog. For most humans, we see the relationship is a positive one, but is that how your dog sees it? What is that relationship built on and how can we improve it?

To answer these questions, we can look at research regarding what matters most in relationships between people. Drs. John and Julie Gottman are professors who have spent 40 years studying over 3,000 couples. Their findings about what matters most for a long-lasting relationship may surprise you.

John Gottman has created a Balance Theory which monitors the type of interactions between partners. To have a successful marriage, you must have five positive interactions for every one negative. These are mostly small. For example, turning toward someone while they are speaking is a positive interaction. Turning away and giving the impression you are not listening when they are speaking is a negative interaction. We may have hundreds of these interactions with each other every day.

John Gottman explains that having a negative interaction is not bad, and it can help us learn to live together better. It is not reasonable to expect that every time we see each other, things will be perfect. However, if the vast majority of these interactions are not positive, the way we feel and interrelate with each other suffers. Although the Gottmans initially started their research to help married couples improve their relationships, their teaching techniques have also been known to help other relationships including parents and friends.

If we get back to thinking about our dogs, what would this Balance Theory look like? Think about the puppy who likes to take the remote control or a loose sock. If we take the object and yell at the puppy who is just being a playful puppy, the interaction will be negative. If we trade a treat for the object with the puppy, we have created a more positive interaction. In the future, the puppy will be more likely to bring you a novel object, rather than run the other direction. Using positive reinforcement training sets you up to have a positive relationship with your dog.

This information is not new and I have not created a new technique to teach dogs more humanely or with more ease. This teaching goes back years, but because as humans we like to look for what is wrong rather than encouraging positive behavior, many people continue to teach dogs using old techniques. Positive reinforcement and force free training is often misunderstood as bribing. If you are consistent and continue using treats, toys, praise, or other desirable things, your dog can learn behaviors so well, that when you cue them to do the behavior, they will respond as if it is a reflex, just like people push the brake when they see a red light.

Once your dog completely understands a behavior, you can reduce the reinforcements to low value and you can give them intermittently. My dog, Captain, loves to sit and he does it nearly 100% of the time. He slows down if he really wants to chase a ball or if we encounter a deer on our walks, but he will still do it. If I need him to sit in the house, he may just get a quick pet or "good boy," but if he has to sit while a herd of deer cross the street in front of us, I give him a hot dog. Sitting while deer cross the street is hard for him. What if your boss stopped paying you for a skill you knew how to do but you dreaded, or what if you did a chore that you hate doing to help your spouse and your spouse said or did nothing? Would you want to do that job for your boss or chore for your spouse next time?

If you've used force free, positive training before, this is all old news to you. However, if you are just starting down the road of positive reinforcement, don't despair. This book teaches you how easy it is to teach your dog without using dominance, discomfort, or dictatorship. Anyone, including me, who has trained for a long time used a choke chain or pinch collar at some point in their life. However, once you understand your dog better, you will see those techniques are no longer needed.

All animals in general, including humans, will repeat anything that results in a positive consequence and will avoid anything that has a negative consequence. Although this is a very general statement, it is true. Animals also understand things that are clearly presented rather than other things that are options. In other words, they like things black or white. They can get confused when things are grey (again, much like humans). By understanding this, we can teach our dogs more effectively when we have clear expectations and are giving clear guidance or instruction. Most of the time our dogs fail or don't understand is because we are not being clear or we are not being consistent.

Dogs and humans have other things in common when learning new skills. We all need motivation and we need to practice. Human motivations are success, money, fun, and other desired outcomes. Dogs don't care about money or specific success, but love treats, fun, and your attention. No matter how great the motivation is, if the new behavior or skill is not practiced, it will not improve. Additionally, the harder the behavior we are asking our dog to perform, the more motivation they may need. Keep this in mind when you are trying to teach your dog to come to you when new smells surround him, such as the first time at a park. If you just have some dry, scentless (low value) dog treats, your dog will likely be overwhelmed with the exciting novel smells and may not respond to you. Picture an opportunity to meet your favorite sports team or music band: would you be able to pay attention to something boring in that overly stimulating environment?

The Biggest Mistakes People Make When Teaching Their Dog

1. **What they are teaching is not clear.**

    This mistake can happen in any part of the teaching process; however, the most common place it happens is with the consequence. If you reinforce a behavior too early or too late, the wrong behavior is reinforced and the desired behavior gets ignored.

    This mistake can also happen when the cue used closely resembles another cue. Either the words or hand signals are so similar that the dog cannot tell the difference and they will often do one behavior for both cues. This commonly happens when people use a hand signal for "sit" and "down." If the two cues are too similar, the dog will default to the behavior that he prefers.

2. **They expect too much too soon.**

    This is probably the most common problem. I often tell people that their dog cannot go directly from kindergarten to college. They must take all the steps in between. For example, they may begin to teach their dog to sit and then expect that they will be able to stay for five minutes right away. People often expect their dogs to behave perfectly in public the first time they leave the house. Dogs need to learn how to behave in public, just as human children learn to do.

Another behavior that people expect too much too soon is with recall or "come." In some cases, they will practice a few times in the house, then take the dog to a park for the first time. When they attempt to call the dog, he does not respond because he is too distracted and does not know the cued behavior well enough to do it in that high distraction environment.

3. **The motivation is not high enough for the expected skill.**

There is often a misunderstanding that dogs should do what we want in order to please us. I am not sure why people think this, since we don't go to work to please our boss. We go to earn money. There are times that we do things to please our partners, spouses, or children, but that is after we have developed a strong relationship, and it is usually something we don't mind doing. There are some things that we teach our dogs that will only require a piece of kibble or another low value treat. If we are teaching a complicated behavior, or if the dog is mildly stressed or distracted, the value of the reinforcement must be higher to keep the dog's attention. If my dog is playing with his dog friends and I want him to come when I call, I need to have a really good reward; otherwise, he will choose fun over my treat.

When I teach the teeter in agility (the piece of equipment that resembles a seesaw), I go very slowly and give a lot of treats. Of all the obstacles in agility, this one tends to cause the most fear because it moves. When I have dogs that are a little afraid of it, I find the highest value treat or toy I can find. When they get on the teeter, they get lots of good things. In some cases, the teeter petrifies some dogs. Once they master it with the high value treats, it becomes a favorite obstacle.

4. **They do not practice long enough to master the skill.**

No matter what the skill or behavior, if we do not practice, we do not improve. Even Olympic athletes have to practice. Dogs are no different. You get out what you put in. If you spend time training your dog every day and increase the challenge in incremental steps, he will master the behavior. If you rarely practice and never increase the challenge, the skill will never improve. It really is that simple.

5. **They only practice in one place and do not increase the level of distraction while teaching.**

This is essentially the same concept as expecting too much too soon. The best way to learn any skill is to first practice when there is little or no distraction. For example, when we learn a new language, we usually start by learning it in a classroom and at home. As we get better, we may begin to practice with friends and family in slightly more distracting environments. Eventually with practice, we can become fluent in a language and speak freely and easily in any environment. It does not happen overnight and it requires practice in a variety of different environments.

Dog Training Made Simple

The following steps make teaching your dog simple. If your dog continues to struggle, be sure you are following the steps precisely. Remember to Keep It Simple, or look at your dog's body language and determine if he is experiencing anxiety or fear (see Body Language, Chapter 5). Just like humans, all dogs will learn at different rates. One behavior will be easy for one dog, but a challenge for another. Anytime your dog feels challenged, make sure they are not anxious or afraid or that you are not expecting too much too soon.

Keeping Things Clear and Simple Is Important for Successful Learning.

▷ No matter how easy or complicated a behavior, you have to start at the beginning. If you want your dog to sit and stay, she must know how to sit before she can sit-stay.

▷ If you want to teach a more complicated behavior like chasing a ball, picking it up with his mouth, bringing the ball to you and dropping it, each behavior is taught individually before you can expect the entire behavior chain.[1]

I-ROAR (Initiate, Request, Observe, Acknowledge, Reward) Steps to Strengthen a Behavior

The **I-ROAR** training technique creates a simple method to use the ABCs of behavior we learned in the last chapter to teach a dog to perform a behavior when cued.

1. **Initiate:** First you must have a way to initiate the behavior you want. You will accomplish this by finding a fun, force free way to get your dog to repeat the behavior. You can lure, shape, target, or capture the behavior such as the way we described luring to teach "sit" in the last chapter.

2. **Request**: Once you have the dog repeating the behavior you want, you can begin requesting the behavior using the cue that you want to

trigger the behavior. This can be a verbal cue or body movement, such as pointing to the floor for lying down.

3. **Observe:** After requesting the behavior, observe to see if your dog performs the desired behavior or begins taking steps that will lead to a desired behavior. Pay attention to your dog so you are clear about the behavior that you want. If your dog does not perform the behavior, go back to luring, shaping, targeting, or capturing the behavior until the dog is consistently performing the behavior. Then start over again with requesting the behavior when you are confident the dog will perform the behavior. While you are observing the behavior, you will want to focus on the accuracy and speed with which your dog responds.

4. **Acknowledge** the desired behavior. Let the dog know he did the desired behavior or started doing the desired behavior by marking the behavior with a click or other marker. For new behaviors, you may acknowledge behaviors that are not "perfect." As your dog practices, you can focus on acknowledging more precise behaviors and ignore less precise attempts.

5. **Reward** the desired behavior. Give your dog a treat or use another reward that he loves to motivate him to want to try the behavior again.

After you mark the correct behavior, make sure you give your dog a reward that represents the appropriate value. If the behavior is hard, use a high value reward. If the behavior is easy or something your dog has already mastered, you can use a less valued reward.

Make sure to use a consistent cue for the behavior. As discussed previously, we want to give clear consistent cues so the dog does not get confused. Then begin using **I-ROAR** to help your dog master the cue by using the following steps.

▷ **I-ROAR** in a low distraction areas. Practice in low distraction places (in the house or backyard) until your dog can consistently perform the behavior on cue. Once your dog performs the behavior on cue reliably, you can use ROAR.

▷ **ROAR** in new places. After you dog has mastered the behavior, practice in new environments, with new distractions to make behavior stronger. (If your dog has difficulty performing the cued behavior in a new environment, try to initiate the behavior a few times the same way when you taught the behavior originally. This should help "remind" your dog of the cued behavior).

▷ **ROAR** with lower value rewards. Once your dog is understanding the new behavior in a variety of environments, you can decrease the value of the rewards you give. For example, you may cue "sit" and begin using verbal praise to acknowledge and reinforce instead of using a clicker and treat.

▷ **ROAR** randomly when the dog masters the behavior. Once your dog completely understands the behavior, you can give a treat, pet, or some other reinforcement randomly.

Although using a clicker is not required during this process, it can help your dog learn faster and easier. The clicker is used to **acknowledge** that the correct behavior was performed, and it is followed by the **reward**.

When starting off trying to **initiate** the behavior you want, avoid using your cue to **request** the behavior. You just want to focus on clicking to **acknowledge** and **reward** any progress your dog makes in performing the behavior you want. At this stage your dog needs to focus on his actions so he can figure out what behavior is getting him the reward. Trying to add a cue while teaching the behavior is equivalent to teaching a football player what plays to run before he has learned to throw the ball or teaching a pianist how to read music before she has learned the keys on the piano.

Once your dog is performing the behavior repetitively and consistently, you can begin to **request** the behavior using your cue. I typically add the cue when I am about 90% sure that my dog will perform the behavior. If you are using a clicker, the same click that **acknowledges** and **rewards** performing the behavior will also **acknowledge** and **reward** the dog for responding to the cue to perform the behavior.

Teaching a New Behavior Using a Clicker

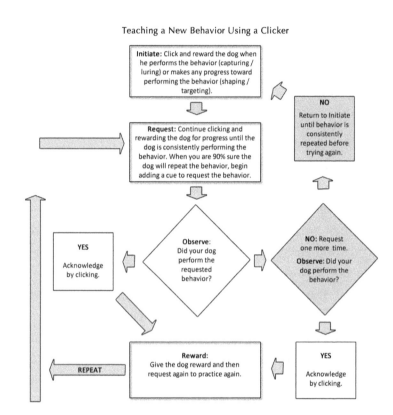

Duration-Distance-Distraction

In order to avoid common mistakes when training your dog, remember these three words: **duration, distance,** and **distraction.** No matter what you teach, you will want to work on all three in order for your dog to master a behavior. I like to use "stay" as an example. At first, we teach a dog to sit, then we add "stay" when we want the dog to stay in the position until we cue another behavior. If we are working on sit-stay, we will have the dog sit and we will stay in front of them for a period of time. I usually start with two to three seconds then cue that the dog can stop performing the behavior, commonly called the "release cue."

Release cues are important because they let the dog know when she is done with the behavior. Otherwise your dog may not know how long she has to stay in place. Commonly used release cues are "all done," "release," "go play," and "alright." Although many people use "ok," I generally recommend against this because "ok" is used often in our everyday language. If you accidentally say it when training, you may inadvertently release your dog from a behavior.

I will gradually work my way up to having the dog stay for 30 seconds while I stand in front of the dog. Once the dog can stay in place for 30 seconds while I am in front of him (**duration**), I will begin to step back, one step at a time (**distance**). Taking baby steps so that the dog succeeds, I gradually increase the **distance** between me and the dog. As the dog is able to stay with me further away, it is time to add **distraction** which can be me marching in place or clapping my hands. Again, I will take baby steps and gradually increase the amount of **distraction**. If a full clap is too distracting and causes the dog to get up from the stay, I will start with a quieter clap. If you consider these words when you are training, you will be far more successful. Eventually I will increase the **distraction** to working in the backyard, then a park.

Training Time/Sessions

We know that people learn best with short sessions. Dogs are the same. Keep your training sessions short (five to ten minutes) and fun. You can have multiple sessions in a day, just make sure you have a good break between them. Studies have shown that learning times can increase if the learner sleeps or plays after a lesson, so consider letting your dog play or take a nap between sessions.

Summary

- To have a positive relationship you need at least five positive interactions for every single negative interaction.

- Common mistakes in training include: Trainers failing because they are not being clear in what they expect, asking too much too soon, using insufficient motivation or reward for the expected skill, failing to practice enough, and failing to practice with distractions.

- Training new cued behaviors can be mastered using **I-ROAR** (Initiate, Request, Observe, Acknowledge, and Reward).

▷ **3 D's** Duration-Distance-Distraction: Practicing cued behaviors for longer durations, at farther distances, and in more distracting places will help solidify the behavior.

▷ Keep your training sessions short and fun.

Eight

Changing an Unwanted Behavior

When my Jack Russell Terrier, Scout, was a puppy, we fed her in the bathroom so the other dogs would not eat her food. In the morning, she ate in the bathroom with me while I got dressed. She would eat her meal from the bowl quickly, then she would jump up and nip my rear end to get my attention. It is hard to ignore a puppy that is nipping your rear end. Because I was getting ready for the day, I could not do a lot of training or give her attention after she ate. Obviously, I needed to find a way to change the behavior. I decided to feed her from a food dispensing toy. (I used a Kibble Nibble ball that I filled with her kibble, and she rolled it around to get the food to fall out). Instead of eating in 30 seconds, it took her about twenty minutes to completely empty the ball. If I was still getting ready, she would lie down on the bath mat and watch me finish instead of nipping me. I was able to provide play time while she ate, so both of her needs got met, and my rear end was safe.

When you are considering changing an unwanted behavior, you first must become a detective. You must determine what happens before or cues the behavior. It is helpful in some situations to figure out when the behavior started, so you can figure out if the dog learned it because the behavior got reinforced or if the dog learned it because he was trying to avoid punishment. In some cases, behaviors learned because of trying to avoid punishment can be more difficult to change and are entwined with fear or anxiety.

Now that you understand how behaviors are learned, let's look at how you can change an unwanted behavior. This will pertain to any normal behavior done at a time or place that you do not want it to occur. If you think your animal is experiencing fear or anxiety or may have a mental disease (like obsessive-compulsive disorder, or separation anxiety severe enough they could hurt themselves, aggression, etc.) or physical illness (urinary tract infection, digestive problem, etc.) or anything that isn't a normal behavior, consult your veterinarian before trying to change the behavior.

Prevent the Undesirable Behavior

The first step to changing an unwanted behavior is to prevent it from occurring. When a dog performs the unwanted behavior, she is practicing it. Not only is she getting better at it, she is creating more muscle memory. Just like we practice piano so our hands will move almost automatically, an unwanted behavior that is practiced will become more ingrained. When preventing a behavior, you may need to block access from the area where it happens or you may need to remove an object from the area if it is triggering your dog. For example, if you want to prevent a dog from jumping on people, you may need to confine the dog to a different room when a person comes to visit or you may need to keep the dog on leash when your dog greets people.

There are many things you can do to prevent unwanted behavior. If you are house training a puppy, you may consider putting her in a crate when you cannot supervise her to prevent her from accidents in the house. If your dog counter surfs, you may need to use a baby gate to restrict access to the area in which she counter surfs. If you have a dog who eats rocks or sticks in the yard, you may need to restrict access to the area or take your dog outside on leash until you can teach him another, more appropriate behavior.

In some situations, dogs will unlearn an unwanted behavior simply by preventing the unwanted behavior for long enough. For example, a dog who has started to eat rocks or bark may forget about eating them if he is prevented from being around them for a period of time if the behavior has not become a strong habit. However, if an unwanted behavior has been practiced by the dog or is highly stimulating, just preventing the behavior for a while may not be enough.

Replace Undesired Behavior with the Desirable One

Another way to try to stop an unwanted behavior is to try teaching an alternative behavior that the dog can do instead of the unwanted behavior. If we go back to the example of a dog jumping on a person, we can teach the dog to sit instead of jumping. First, you will need to teach the dog to sit with the three D's (distance, duration and distraction). Once the dog knows how to stay seated during an exciting/distracting event, the dog can then be allowed to approach a person while he is on leash. When the dog gets closer to the person, cue him to sit. If he sits, the person can give him treats and attention (consequence = something desired). If he does not sit and stay seated, the visitor should walk away and ignore the dog (consequence = something undesired). If the dog has a hard time at first, you can cue him to sit while farther away from the person and you can treat him to reduce the excitement. Then you can gradually work closer. It is important to keep the dog on leash during this process so the dog cannot practice jumping on the person.

It is important to think of a behavior you would like the dog to do in the specific situation. When we are house-training a puppy, we keep the puppy in a crate when she cannot be supervised. When she is out of the crate, we take her outside to go potty. When she finishes, we give her a treat so she knows that going potty in the yard is appropriate and desired. Eventually, the puppy knows where to go potty and is no longer crated to prevent accidents.

For puppies that are house training, dogs that counter surf, or dogs that eat rocks and sticks, this is the time you gradually give them more access or the ability to try. If they are successful, you can give them more freedom. If they make a mistake, it means they need more practice and you will need to go back to preventing and training the new behavior.

Another Example

Let's say that your dog will not come back to you when you let her off leash at the beach. You will need to keep her on leash at the beach or avoid the beach completely at first. At home or in low distracting areas, you would need to practice recall until it is very reliable. Once she will come to you in low distraction areas, you will begin to add distraction. You may also need to keep her on a long line at first. Once you feel like you have a reliable recall by training in the backyard, front yard, then quiet park, you may venture back to the beach.

On your first visit back to the beach, you would want to practice recall on a long line, so if she got distracted, she could not get away from you. Once she focuses on you and becomes reliable on the long line, you could try having her off leash.

There are some situations when unwanted behavior is more rewarding than anything you can offer. In these situations, you may always have to prevent or manage the unwanted behavior. When you are working with behaviors that are motivating within themselves, like running on the beach or chasing birds, you must find an extremely valuable reward in order to teach your dog to stop the other behavior and do the behavior you prefer. Changing behavior is difficult. Whenever possible, prevention is always the best way to go.

When Emotions Affect Behavior

Some behaviors are the result of anxiety, fear, or excitement. As mentioned before, if a learner is too stressed, learning cannot occur. If the anxiety or fear is mild, you can help your dog with some homeopathic therapies. Some of these therapies can help if you have a high-energy puppy or dog because they calm them down enough so they can learn the behaviors you are trying to teach.

Thundershirt. This is a dog shirt that fits tightly on the dog's body. It comes from the same reasoning that we use when we swaddle a baby. The tightness can help calm the nervous system and allow the dog to be present when learning. The thundershirt can also be used during fireworks or thunderstorms.

Adaptil Pheromones. These pheromones come in collars, diffusers, and sprays. In some cases, these pheromones help reduce fear and anxiety so the dog can learn with less stress.

Through a Dog's Ear (and other classical music created to calm dogs). This music was specifically created to calm dogs. You can use this when training; however, it is more beneficial to use when the dogs are relaxing on their own.

Supplements (Zylkene, Anxitane). Daily supplements were created to help mildly anxious or stressed dogs. For some dogs, this daily supplement can help reduce stress and allow them to learn more easily. You should ask your veterinarian if these supplements may help your dog.

Desensitization and Counter Conditioning (Fear to Fun)

Additionally, if the dog's behavior comes from fear, anxiety, or stress, processes called desensitization and counter conditioning might help change the dog's emotional response to the situation. **Desensitization** is a behavior modification technique where an undesirable emotional response (usually fear) to a given stimulus is reduced or extinguished by repeatedly exposing the subject to that stimulus. For example, if a dog is afraid of skateboards, the dog could be put in a backyard with a skateboard just sitting on the ground. At first the dog may be afraid, but after a while he would probably get used to the skateboard. The dog would get used to or desensitized to the skateboard.

Counter conditioning is another form of behavior modification that involves the changing of a negative response to a stimulus into a positive response by the association of positive actions with the stimulus. Teaching dogs to use the tunnel in agility, which I explained earlier in the book, is a good example of this. Agility tunnels are manufactured using collapsible fabric and are six to eighteen feet long at their full length. Many dogs are initially afraid to go through them.

To help fearful dogs to go through the tunnel, I collapse the tunnel until it is maybe a foot in length. Then I treat the dog generously for going through it. Some dogs will still be afraid of going through even the shortened tunnel. In those cases, we treat the dog initially for looking at or even just going near the tunnel. Then they receive treats for getting closer and eventually sticking their heads in the tunnel. After enough rewards, the dogs begin to learn that the tunnel is something that gives them rewards and is not scary. Once the dog begins going through the shortened tunnel, I begin to stretch out the tunnel until it is full length. In the end, I take something that started as fearful and make it fun.

During this process, it is important not to push or force your dog. If I push a dog through the tunnel, I risk turning the event into a punishment or risk putting the dog over the threshold and I could trigger a fight, flight, or freeze response. For example, if the dog stops taking treats, tries to run away, or starts to freeze, I know I have pushed them too far. In that case, I will just back farther away from the tunnel, maybe take a break. Then I slowly start the process over and always try to end positively.

Depending on the fear level of the dog, this whole process may take a few sessions. After over ten years of using this technique in agility classes, I have never had a dog that I have not been able to teach to go through a full length tunnel. The great thing about this process is that once a fearful dog has learned to master the tunnel even moderately, the dog is often more willing to try other new things with their handler's help in the future.

If your dog is experiencing extreme anxiety, fear, or stress, you should consult a professional to help. The therapies above work for some dogs but do not seem to affect others. They are used to help your dog learn but should be avoided if your dog needs medical attention.

Seeing a Behaviorist or Someone Who Specializes in Behavior.

Chapter 10 will explain these professionals in detail. He or she may recommend medication to help with the fear or anxiety. Unfortunately, our society has a lot of negative thoughts about medications to help brain diseases like fear and anxiety. We see these thoughts in human medicine so much so that people suffer from depression, anxiety, bipolar disorder, and many other brain diseases because they feel ashamed of taking the medication. This is frustrating to me because people will take medications for other illness and diseases without a concern. People take antibiotics for an infection, insulin for diabetes, chemotherapy for cancer, and aspirin to reduce a heart attack or headache, but there is a lot of shame if they need a medication to help their brain. If your dog is experiencing fear or anxiety and the professional recommends a medication, please consider it for the health of your dog. In many situations, the medication is temporary if you follow the behavior modification plan they provide. The medication will calm him enough so he can learn and once he learns a new way, he can often stop taking the medication.

Summary

▷ Determine what triggers the unwanted behavior.

▷ Prevent the unwanted behavior from happening.

▷ Teach a new, more desirable behavior.

▷ Replace the old behavior with the new behavior.

▷ Emotions can positively or negatively affect behavior.

▷ Consider using supplements or medication to help reduce the fear or anxiety so your dog can learn faster.

Nine

Teaching the Humans

When I met Marcy and her black lab mix Bella, she had worked with three other trainers, none of which helped her with Bella's issues. Marcy was leery of positive reinforcement, but I came highly recommended by a friend. (This type of client is often a lot of work at the beginning but ends up being very rewarding). The three main issues that Marcy had with Bella were that she pulled on leash, she refused to come when called, and she would not let anyone touch her head. At our first meeting, Bella exhibited almost every sign of fear and anxiety immediately.

This was one of the only clients that I stopped during our introductions to explain her dog's body language to her. Bella's tail was tucked. She was cowering, her ears pressed back as far as possible, and she was panting and licking her lips. As I continued to watch her during the appointment, she yawned, sniffed, and paced. She was very nervous and afraid. As I watched her, I also noticed that she was wearing a pinch collar. I explained to Marcy that I did not use pinch collars and explained why.

I explained to Marcy that the pinch collar could actually be making all of the behaviors worse, which is why the other three traditional trainers were not able to help. I told her that I thought Bella was scared on walks and the pinch collar was adding pain to an already scary situation. I also explained that the pinch collar could be contributing to her dislike of her head being touched since you had to put it over her head to put it on.

Although Marcy was resistant to using a harness, she finally agreed. Getting the harness over Bella's head did take some coaxing and a lot of very high value treats. The first three weeks of training were a little rough because Marcy would cheat and occasionally walked Bella using the pinch collar. I tried to explain that she was actually slowing down the training when she cheated. During the fourth or fifth session, I was sitting in a chair when Bella approached me as I was talking with Marcy. Bella sat next to me while we talked, and I started to pet her behind her ears. She did not move away and actually moved into my touch. Eventually, I was petting her head, and she was not moving away. Marcy and I were both surprised, and Marcy told me that no one had been able to do that. This gave me the opportunity to explain that Bella had only experienced positive things with me, therefore she likely trusted me more. Although this made Marcy sad, she finally realized that she was causing some of Bella's fear.

After that session, Marcy never used the pinch collar again. We continued to work together a few more months and when Bella finally graduated, Marcy thanked me. She was in tears, *and she told me that I not only helped with the unwanted behaviors, I also helped mend their relationship.*

When I am working with my clients, at some point they eventually realize that I am not actually teaching their dogs, I am teaching them how to teach their dogs. I admit that working with a dog who is experiencing fear, anxiety, or who is barking, growling, or lunging may be more challenging, but teaching your dog the basics is not as complicated. In addition, once you understand the basics of how to teach your dog, helping them in fearful situations will be easier. I work with dogs who just need to learn manners, dogs that bite, and everything in between.

With all of the dogs and people I have met, I have never met a bad dog and I have never met a bad person. I have met many dogs that exhibit bad or inappropriate behavior and I have met many people who don't know what to do in those situations. I often compare it to a parent who has a child that had severe ADHD, Autism, Asperger's, or another brain disease. The parents are not bad because they have these children. They just need help figuring out how best to help their children. Asking for help is hard to do, but it is the best thing to do when you love your dog or child.

The most challenging thing about teaching humans is to get them to accept that there are other ways to do things if they have trained dogs before. Humans and dogs are creatures of habit, and it becomes uncomfortable to learn something new even if the old way is not working, like in the case of childbed fever and the Semmelweis Reflex. For many people, traditional training with choke, pinch, or electric collars is all they have ever known. Dog training also has a history of misinformation about dogs being just like wolves or that dogs seek to dominate humans. Unfortunately, the years of misinformation is clouding the science-based information that we have to show that dogs differ greatly from wolves, and they are not seeking dominance over humans. Over the years, we have moved away from teachers hitting students with rulers and therapists using shock therapy on people, but we still use these aversive techniques on dogs when it is unnecessary.

Being a beginner at anything is hard, whether you are a human or a dog or if you are an adult or a child. However, we are always learning; therefore, we will always be a beginner if we want to make improvements in our life. A beginner opens himself to learning new things and we must Practice. Practice. Practice. It is also extremely important to exercise patience with yourself and your dog.

Using treats, markers, or clickers may seem new to you and that is okay. Being willing to take this journey will not only open your mind but it will improve your relationship with your dog and possibly others in your life too. When you stop looking for what is bad and start embracing the good, your whole life can change. Traditional training looks for the "no" in behavior so it can be corrected. Positive, force free training is looking for the "yes." Dogs and humans both respond better to praise, rewards, gifts, and bonuses than criticism, complaints, and punishment. When you start training your dog, strengthening your bond and trust is an opportunity. In many cases, I noticed that when the dog begins to have fun with training, the person has fun as well.

When you start training your dog, you may experience a time when you think your dog knows better but continues to do the unwanted behavior. If this occurs, it is important to see how you are responding to the unwanted behavior.

People often struggle with dogs jumping on them. They will tell me that they tell their dog to get off or get down and they do not respond. When this occurs, there are a few things that are happening. Sometimes in these situations, our dog perceives negative attention as better than no attention. For these dogs, your reprimand may be viewed as a reward. This is why is it is best to ignore unwanted behaviors, that means *completely ignore*, no eye contact, no laughing, no talking. Other times we give our dogs mixed signals if we have not been consistent in what we are asking. If sometimes you laugh and scratch your dog when he jumps on you, but you get mad at the dog when he jumps on strangers, you are giving the dog mixed messages.

Another common mistake people make is to use the word "down" for lie on your stomach, and they use "down" to tell their dog to not jump or get off furniture. When you are teaching your dog, consider creating a "dog dictionary" with detailed description of what you want the dog to do for each cue. Personally, I use "down" to cue my dog to lay on his stomach, and I use "off" to mean all four feet are on the ground, whether they jump on me or are on a couch that is off limits.

There are some behaviors that our dogs do when we are not home. When this happens, people get very frustrated since they cannot redirect the behavior when they are absent. As humans, we can control the environment. If your dog consistently counter surfs when you are home, you have two easy options. You can make sure there is nothing on the counter so the dog does not get a reward like a loaf of bread or box of cookies, or you can prevent your dog from having access to the kitchen when you cannot supervise. When unwanted behaviors occur when we are not at home, prevention or management is the best option.

It is important to realize that actions are louder than words. If you physically punish your dog for a behavior, he is more likely to remember the punishment than that you verbally said "I love you." As mentioned above, negative attention is better than no attention. If you decide to ignore an unwanted behavior but you reinforce a wanted behavior with treats, toys or praise, it is more likely that your dog will repeat the reinforced behavior. If you punish your dog for an unwanted behavior, you are still giving them attention, so your reinforcement for a desired behavior is less noticed.

It is also important that we avoid labeling our dogs. I have noticed that sometimes people label their dogs as dumb, stubborn, unmotivated, etc. When we label others (including people), we often unintentionally put them into a box. In many cases, this box puts limits on what we think we can teach them or what we think they can learn. More often than not, these labels are not true. Labeling never benefits anyone.

Consider what happens when we label humans as the smart one, the stupid one, the wild one. Whether the label is a compliment or a criticism, it often puts the labeled person in a box and they often are unable to change. Labels create unnecessary limits or expectations. Every day we see people and animals who have been labeled with a disability do amazing things. Nick Vujicic is a man who does not have arms or legs but he travels the world speaking to groups, and he has written *Stand Strong: You Can Overcome Bullying (and Other Stuff That Keeps You Down*. He did not let his disability or any labels hold him back. There are dogs and cats that are born without front or back limbs but they still walk and thrive. Labels only create limits, and there is no benefit to that.

My experience as a dog trainer has taught me that any dog is capable of doing more than we think. It is only our beliefs and thoughts that limit us and them. Of course, some dogs may have physical limitations and some breeds will excel at something more than others, but if we keep an open mind, we can accomplish a lot more. In my agility classes, one of the fastest, most skilled agility dogs is a French Bulldog. He is fast, he is a great jumper, and he is superb at the weave poles. It is my belief that any dog can do any skill. Of course, some will be more successful than others, but that is the same with people. We cannot all be Olympic athletes.

When you are training your dog, it is important to remember that both of you are learning. Even if you have trained dogs before, each time you train a new dog, you are both learning. As a professional, I treat every dog and human as an individual, and just because one technique works for one, it may not work for another. It is important that you show patience to yourself and your dog. If you are in a bad or stressful mood, you may decide not to train your dog at that time. Be sure that you are aware that if you are experiencing anxiety or fears, your dog may notice and become warier. When you begin to work with your dog on a regular basis, they will learn your mood and will become a true partner.

Training using force-free, positive techniques can create a beautiful, unbreakable bond.

Summary

▷ There are no bad dogs or bad humans—just inappropriate behavior.

▷ Get help when needed.

▷ Look for the "yes" when training.

▷ Pay attention to what you are asking for and what you are reinforcing.

▷ When dogs are alone, prevent or manage unwanted behavior.

▷ Avoid labels.

▷ Be patient with yourself and your dog.

Ten

Finding a Behaviorist or Trainer When You Need Help

Hopefully, you now have an improved understanding of what training is and what it is not, and you realize that dogs experience emotions that are similar to ours. Dogs are also like us because they sometimes need more help. When we train our dogs, we are their teachers, just as humans have teachers in schools. We are teaching them new behaviors so we can help them live in our world. We are teaching them right from wrong. We are teaching them games and sports. In this way, we are being both parent and teacher. There may be times when your dogs will need more than a parent or teacher, just as humans sometimes do.

Just like humans, there are times that dogs need to go to a therapist or psychiatrist. If you are concerned that your dog may be experiencing severe fear, anxiety, or have a mental disease, it is time to consider looking for additional help.

If you are fortunate enough to have a Veterinary Behaviorist in your area,[1] that is a great place to start. A veterinary behaviorist is a veterinarian that has done additional schooling to specialize in behavior (like surgeons, radiologists, oncologists, and other veterinary specialists). These veterinarians can help with things from separation anxiety to obsessive-compulsive disorder and everything in between. A veterinary behaviorist may recommend medication to help if your dog is suffering from a mental disease. Dogs can have many of the mental diseases that affect people. When you go to a specialist, he or she will likely give you a behavior modification plan. Behavior modification is similar to getting therapy to help with the specific problem from which your dog is suffering. The behavior modification works for managing or changing the problem. Like humans, medications for mental disease work best when they work in tandem with therapy, just as a person on Prozac for depression should go to a therapist.

Unfortunately, there are very few veterinary behaviorist in the world, so you may not have one in the area. If this is the case, you can also look for other types of behaviorist (CAAB is a Certified Applied Animal Behaviorist)[2] or trainers that have training in working with these issues. These professionals cannot prescribe medications, but they often work with general practice veterinarians that are knowledgeable about mental disease drugs. They will be able to help with a behavior modification plan. If you find a trainer who is able to help with behavior modification, be sure you look into their training and philosophy before you work with them. Here are a

few things you should find out before you hire a trainer for
behavior modification:

▷ They should only use positive, force-free techniques.

▷ Their education should include training that is above and
  beyond basic animal training. Remember, behavior modification is not training. It is more like therapy, so you
  want assurance that you are working with a therapist, not
  a teacher. In addition to books, the trainer should attend
  continuing education conferences on a regular basis.

▷ They should respect your dog and you.

▷ They should teach you how to manage and work with
  your dog so you have skills to take home.

▷ They should refer you to a specialist or veterinarian who
  understands behavior if the issue gets worse or does not
  improve.

Hopefully your animals will never experience a mental
disease, but since animals live in our crazy world, if you have
a lot of animals, it is likely one may need a little extra help.
As they say, knowledge is power, so if you can recognize that
something is not right, you will be able to help your animal a
lot faster than if you did not understand.

If you find that you are in need of a professional, go to the
Appendix to see how you can find someone near you.

About
Shannon Coyner

Shannon has been a pet lover all her life and a dog trainer for over 20 years. She has spent her life observing, caring for, and training animals of all kinds. She has worked in the Bird Department at Marine World Africa USA, and worked as a handler and trainer for an African Serval Cat at Safari West, a private zoo in Santa Rosa, California. In college, she participated in behavior studies including observations of bald eagles and Addax antelopes through the San Francisco Zoo and Safari West.

She also has an extensive background working in the veterinary field. She worked for ten years in veterinary clinics as a Registered Veterinary Technician. Eventually, she was promoted to office manager and head technician in a clinic managing three veterinarians and their staff. During this time she developed puppy classes in the veterinary clinic and helped develop other behavioral training methods into the practice.

Shannon is deeply interested in the science behind animal behavior. In 2011 to 2012, she interned with Veterinary Behaviorist Dr. Rachel Malamed. She is one of the few veterinary technician graduates of the North American Veterinary Professional Institute Behavior Course presented by Dr. Karen Overall, Dr. Kersti Seksel, and Dr. Martin Godbout, taking the course in 2012 and 2016. In 2014 she completed Living and Learning with Animals (LLA) for veterinary and other animal behavior professionals, by Dr. Susan Friedman. Shannon has served as President for the Society of Veterinary Behavior Technicians.

As a dog trainer, Shannon spent many years as the head dog trainer for PAWS for Healing, a pet-assisted therapy organization. She performed temperament testing and assisted in the training of therapy dogs who visited hospitals, veteran groups, special educational facilities, and convalescent homes. She believes strongly in the benefits of developing the human-animal bond.

She founded Ventura Pet Wellness and Dog Training Center in 2006. The center offers a variety of training classes and Shannon offers private training lessons for more complex behavior problems. She specializes in helping fearful and unsocialized dogs. In 2015, she also developed Truly Force Free Animal Training, an Internet-based training site dedicated to spreading knowledge regarding force free training.

As a speaker, Shannon has taught animal first aid and an introductory course regarding becoming a veterinary technician. She has taught a Behavior and Handling Workshop at Pima Community College, Tucson, Arizona, for the veterinary technician program. She has also presented multiple seminars regarding canine body language and canine learning.

Her education includes a Biology Degree, specializing in Zoology from Sonoma State University. She is a Registered Veterinary Technician, a Certified Professional Dog Trainer, a Karen Pryor Academy Certified Training Partner, a member of the Association of Pet Professional Dog Trainers, member of the Pet Professional Guild, and a member of the International Association of Animal Behavior Consultants.

Acknowledgments

- To all the dogs, cats, birds, horses and any other animal that I have been able to learn from and that, hopefully, live extraordinary lives themselves

- Jeff—for supporting me, giving me space to write and taking on extra chores

- Riley—for being excited that I can help animals in another way

- Shawn—for believing that his mom can do anything she sets her mind to

- Cole—for being my constant cheerleader in every aspect of my life

- Jan & Gary—for allowing me to use their lake house as a retreat and a place to write

- Mom & Dad—for supporting my dream to work with animals

- Grandpa—for always being interested and excited about the things I do

▷ Pat & Jamie—who helped me "deliver" this child that has been in me for far too long (Bookectomy.com)

▷ Terri—for her continual support and enthusiasm, without whome Truly Force Free and this book would not exist

▷ Melissa—who helped me keep Ventura Pet Wellness organized and running while I focused on the book AND for helping me keep my life organized and less stressful

▷ Emily—who always knew I would do it and NEVER doubted my ability

▷ Karisa—for being that friend that you can say anything to and she will always love you

▷ Captain & Scout—for laying by my feet (or on the bed) patiently while I wrote—even when they wanted to hike and swim when we were at the lake

▷ David (from heaven)—for being the angel that made me realize that life can change in an instant and you never know if tomorrow will come (although I wish with all of my heart that I could have learned this a different way so he would still be here today)

▷ Karen Overall—who was the speaker of the first veterinary behavior lecture I ever attended (when I knew I wanted to be more than just a veterinary technician and dog trainer)

▷ Rachel Malamed—who strengthened my behavior knowledge

▷ Shane & Lorinda—who supported me in following my passion for behavior in the veterinary clinic

▷ The Hoffman Institute (with special thanks to Ed McClune and Linda Newlin)—who helped me live an authentic life, taught me that I am a spiritual being, gave me the confidence that I could do anything I set out to, taught me how to a create vision for my life beyond what I could have ever imagined, and taught me how to live a happy, joyful life

▷ Lyme disease and its disease cousins—if I had never gotten sick, I would not have slowed down enough to create TFF and this book, which gave me more empathy and compassion than I ever thought possible and for forcing me to look at less physical ways to get my word out to the world which has led me to help more animals than I could if I only did my "physical" job

▷ Dr. Laufer—who diagnosed and treated the Lyme and co-infections so I could get my life back

▷ Cerebrum Medical Center—who diagnosed and treated the head traumas that were preventing me from getting better

As I write this I am realizing that I would need to thank everyone who ever touched my life (good or bad) because it led me to the place I am now. If I had made a different decision or choice, if I had not met that one person (even if it was just a quick discussion with the men at the antique store in Paso Robles or the woman who gave me a bag at the store so

I did not have to purchase one), my life could be drastically different.

Thank you all for being in my life, in any way that you were/are, because you led me to where I am today.

Lastly, I would like to thank God for putting me on this path and I would like to apologize for those really hard days that I cursed at you.

Endnotes

Introduction:

1. Wolfs, F. Introduction to the scientific method. Physics Laboratory Experiments, Appendix E, Department of

2. Stuart Clark, Are great scientists always heretics?, BBC Science, April 11, 2013 http://www.bbc.co.uk/science/0/22078983

3. Imre Zoltan, Ignaz Semmelweis, Britannica Biography, last updated 10/28/2016 https://www.britannica.com/biography/Ignaz-Semmelweis

4. Rebecca Davis, The Doctor Who Championed Hand-Washing and Briefly Saved Lives, National Public Radio, January 12, 2015 http://www.npr.org/sections/health-shots/2015/01/12/375663920/the-doctor-who-championed-hand-washing-and-saved-women-s-lives

5. Zoltan

6. Jim Taylor, Cognitive Biases v.s. Common Sense –Can you resist the pull of cognitive biases?, Psychology Today, 2011 https://www.psychologytoday.com/blog/the-power-prime/201107/cognitive-biases-vs-common-sense

Chapter 1:

1. Cesar Millan, Balancing the equation, https://www.cesarsway.com/cesar-millan/cesars-blog/balancing-the-equation

2. Ed Frawley, The problem with all positive dog training, https://leerburg.com/allpositive.htm

3. Lauren Davis, Why everything you know about wolf packs is wrong, (11/28/2014) Gizmodo io9. http://io9.gizmodo.com/why-everything-you-know-about-wolf-packs-is-wrong-1664301968

4. L. David Mech What Ever Happened to the Term Alpha Wolf?, International Wolf, The Quarterly Publication of the International Wolf Center, Volume 19, No. 4 Winter 2008.

5. Id.

6. Id.

7. Bradshaw, J.W.S., Blackwell, E.J. and Casey, R.A., Dominance in domestic dogs – useful construct or bad habit? Journal of Veterinary Behavior, Clinical Applications and Research, Volume 4, Issue 3, Pages 109-144 (May-June 2009)

8. Saul McLeod, Skinner- Operant Conditioning, Simply Psychology, published 2007, updated 2015 http://www.simplypsychology.org/operant-conditioning.html

9. Operant conditioning also includes positive punishment, negative punishment and negative reinforcement. The technical meanings of these descriptions can be extremely confusing as Skinner's use of the words positive, negative, reinforcement and punishment do not align with their ordinary everyday usage. For the purpose of this book, I am avoiding the technical terms to avoid confusion.

10. McLeod.

11. Id.

12. Sophia Yin, The Best Animal Trainers in History: Interview with Bob and Marian Bailey, Part 1, August 13, 2012, https://drsophia-yin.com/blog/entry/the-best-animal-trainers-in-history-interview-with-bob-and-marian-bailey/

13. See Murray A. Straus et al., Spanking by Parents and Subsequent Antisocial Behavior of Children, 151 ARCHIVES OF PEDIATRICS & ADOLESCENT MED. 761, (1997) (noting studies finding links between corporal punishment and behavioral problems such as depression, anxiety, low self-esteem, and aggressive/delinquent behavior).

14. American Veterinary Society of Animal Behavior Position Statement, The Use of Punishment for Behavior Modification in Animals, citing Azrin NH, Rubin HB, Hutchinson RR. 1968. Biting attack by rats in response to aversive shock. J Exp Anal Behav 11: 633-639.

15. Id. citing Hutchinson RR. 1977. By-products of aversive control. In: Honig WK, Staddon JER, eds. Handbook of Operant behavior. Englewood Cliffs, NJ: Prentice-Hall: 415-431 and Azrin NH. 1960. Effects of punishment intensity during variable-interval reinforcement. J Exp Anal Behav 3: 123-142.

16. Id citing Pauli AM, Bentley E, Diehl AK, Miller PE. 2006. Effects of the application of neck pressure by a collar or harness on intraocular pressure in dogs. J Am Anim Hosp Assoc 42(3): 207-211 and Drobatz KJ, Saunders HM, Pugh CR, Hendricks JC. 1995. Noncardiogenic pulmonary edema in dogs and cats: 26 cases (1987-1993). J Am Vet Med Assoc 206: 1732-1736.

17. Matthijs B.H. Schilder, Joanne A.M. van der Borg, Training dogs with the help of the shock collar: short and long term behavioral effects, Applied Animal Behavior Science 85 (2004) 319-334.

18. Id.

19. Mardi Richmond, Guide Dogs For the Blind: Guide Dogs for the Blind changes training methods, and the results are amazing. http://thebark.com/content/guide-dogs-blind

20. Ruth Lysons, Nick Coulson, A review of Recent Evidence in Relation to the Welfare Implications for Cats and Dogs Arising from the Use of Electronic Collars, Welsh Government commissioned an independent review of recent evidence in relation to the welfare implications for cats and dogs arising from the use of electronic collars. November 16, 2015.

21. Cooper J, Cracknell N, Hardiman J, Wright H and Mills D, 2014, The Welfare Consequences and Efficacy of Training Pet Dogs with Remote Electronic Training Collars in Comparison to Reward Based Training, PLos One 9(9).

22. A preliminary study on this same project found increased cortisol levels (a known stress hormone) in dogs trained using electronic collars compared to those using positive reinforcement techniques, but was criticized because the trainers did not necessarily use

the factory recommendations of the shock collar manufacturers. Therefore, for this study only trainers approved by the manufacturers association were used.

23. Dutton; Painter (1981). Traumatic Bonding: The development of emotional attachments in battered women and other relationships of intermittent abuse. Victimology: An International Journal (7).

24. Franklin D. McMillan, DVM, DACVIM, (2003) A World of Hurts-Is Pain Special?, Journal of the American Veterinary Medical Association, Vol 223, No. 2, July 15, 2003

Chapter 2:

1. Brandon Keim, Brain Scans Show Striking Similarities Between Dogs and Humans, February 20, 2014 https://www.wired.com/2014/02/dog-brains-vocal-processing/; Andics A1, Gácsi M2, Faragó T2, Kis A3, Miklósi A4., Voice-sensitive regions in the dog and human brain are revealed by comparative fMRI. Curr Biol. 2014 Mar 3;24(5):574-8. doi: 10.1016/j.cub.2014.01.058. Epub 2014 Feb 20.

2. Nicola Davis, Secret of connection between dogs and humans could be genetic, September 29, 2016, https://www.theguardian.com/science/2016/sep/29/secret-of-connection-between-dogs-and-humans-could-be-genetic; M.E. Persson et al. 2016. Genomic Regions Associated With Interspecies Communication in Dogs Contain Genes Related to Human Social Disorders. Sci. Rep. 6: 33439; doi: 10.1038/srep33439

3. Jane J. Lee, Dog and Human Genomes Evolved Together, May 14, 2013, http://news.nationalgeographic.com/news/2013/13/130514-dogs-domestication-humans-genome-science/; Wang GD, et al. The genomics of selection in dogs and the parallel evolution between dogs and humans. Nat Commun. 2013;4:1860.

4. Michael Casey, Dogs and people bond through eye contact, April 17, 2015 http://www.cbsnews.com/news/dogs-and-people-bond-through-eye-contact/; Miho Nagasawa, et al. Oxytocin-gaze positive loop and the coevolution of human-dog bonds, Science 17 Apr 2015:Vol. 348, Issue 6232, pp. 333-336.

5. Katharina C. Kirchhofer et al. Dogs (Canis familiaris), but Not Chimpanzees (Pan troglodytes), Understand Imperative Pointing. PLoS ONE, 2012; 7 (2): e30913 DOI: 10.1371/journal.pone.0030913

6. , SFGate Newspaper, October 2006.

7. AVSAB, Position Statement on the Use of Dominance Theory in Behavior Modification of Animals, 2008 https://avsab.org/wp-content/uploads/2016/08/Dominance_Position_Statement_download-10-3-14.pdf. Even the few scientists that believe that dominance has some use in describing the hierarchy of dogs in social groups recommend against enforcing dominant status by humans because of the considerable risk of injury. M.B.H. Schilder, et al. Dominance in domestic dogs revisited: Useful habit and useful construct? (2014) J VET BEHAV 9, 184-191.

Chapter 3:

1. R. K. Anderson letter, used with permission. Canine and Feline Behavior for Veterinary Technicians and Nurses, First Edition. Edited by Julie K. Shaw and Debbie Martin. © 2015 John Wiley & Sons, Inc. Published 2015 by John Wiley & Sons, Inc. Companion Website: www.wiley.com/go/shaw/behavior

2. Anna Pukas, Play with your pooch: The secret to your dog's happiness, Life & Style (December 12, 2014). http://www.express.co.uk/life-style/life/547030/Secret-dog-s-happiness

3. Stanley Coren, What Dogs Do After Training Affects How Much They Remember, Psychology Today (October 26, 2016). https://www.psychologytoday.com/blog/canine-corner/201610/what-dogs-do-after-training-affects-how-much-they-remember

Chapter 4:

1. Ellie Zolfagharifard, How the direction of a tail wag could reveal your dog's MOOD: To the right and they're happy - but to the left they could be scared, Daily Mail, 31 October 2013 Updated: 1 November 2013. http://www.dailymail.co.uk/sciencetech/article-2481634/How-direction-tail-wag-reveal-dogs-MOOD.html; Marcello Siniscalch, et al. Seeing Left- or Right-Asymmetric Tail Wagging Produces Different Emotional Responses in Dogs, Current Biology, Volume 23, Issue 22, p2279–2282, 18 November 2013.

2. Association of Pet Dog Trainers, UK; Miles Anita, Dissertation-Pathologies of the Dog Associated with the Use of Choke Chains, European School of Animal Osteopathy, 2007.

Chapter 5:

1. https://www.dognition.com/

Chapter 7:

1. A behavior chain is a group of behaviors that occur in a sequence and are linked together by learned cues.

Chapter 10:

1. https://avsab.org/resources/speakers-bureau behavior-consultants-near-you/

2. http://www.animalbehaviorsociety.org/web/applied-behavior-caab-directory.php

CPSIA information can be obtained
at www.ICGtesting.com
Printed in the USA
BVHW08s2248310518
517872BV00007B/157/P

9 780999 284605